D1453332

THE TILLMAN MOVEMENT IN SOUTH CAROLINA

TILLMAN AS GOVERNOR

THE TILLMAN MOVEMENT IN SOUTH CAROLINA

BY

FRANCIS BUTLER SIMKINS

Assistant Professor of History in Emory University

GLOUCESTER, MASS.

PETER SMITH

1964

TO

GILBERTO FREYRE

A foreign friend who taught me to appreciate the past
of my native state

PREFACE

This study seeks to tell of the most significant transformation that has affected the political life of South Carolina since Reconstruction; namely, the passing of the control of the state from the hands of Wade Hampton and the men who surrounded him into the hands of Ben Tillman and his farmer friends. While there is danger of overemphasizing the social significance of this transfer of power, for in fact Hampton and Tillman both were ever loyal Democrats believing the whites should rule to the exclusion of the Negro; nevertheless, there was a fundamental social difference which made the rivalry of these men something more than personal. Hampton believed in the rule of the white democracy through a leadership derived from the social system which existed before the Civil War; whereas Tillman believed in the rule of the white democracy through the leadership of a new generation, which had arisen as the result of social changes after 1865.

I have found it convenient to approach the study of this topic through the personality of Tillman, as I feel that Tillman, in his life and work, embodied the spirit of this transference of leadership. Yet no attempt has been made to produce a biography of Tillman, for biographical matter is subordinated to the general narrative of the so-called Tillman Movement. With this purpose as a guide, the work begins with a description of politics in South Carolina after Reconstruction and with an attempt to show why the overthrow of the régime established in 1877 was inevitable; then follows a description of the early life and influences of Tillman, his advent into the politics of the state, his ideas of reform; later comes the story of his attempts at reform through others, followed by his own successful candidacy for governor, his administrative methods, and the constructive reforms which he accomplished. The study closes with an attempt to estimate the influence of Tillman upon South Carolina after he became United States senator and after his death.

In the preparation of this work the author has received the kind assistance of Mr. B. R. Tillman, the eldest son of the principal character in this study, who has given him free access to the papers in the Tillman Library at Trenton. Among the many who have given first-hand information concerning events of which they were eye witnesses, or have pointed out sources of information, the following should be mentioned: Professor Yates Snowden and Mr. R. M. Kennedy, of the University of South Carolina; the Honorable Eugene B. Gary, Chief Justice of South Carolina, Colonel

John R. Abney, of New York City; Mr. Thomas Kirkland, of Kershaw; Dr. C. P. DeVore, of Edgefield; Mr. A. S. Salley, Jr., Secretary of the South Carolina Historical Commission; and the author's deceased kinsman, Dr. Francis W. P. Butler, of Columbia. My young friend and fellow student, Robert White Linker, of Salisbury, North Carolina, has lent his keen judgment in the preparation of the work. Professor J. E. Walmsley, of Farmville, Virginia, has been of great aid in the preparation of the maps. Among those who have given invaluable critical suggestion in the revision of the text are: Reverend Herbert Boyce Satcher, of Philadelphia; Professor J. M. Ariail, of Columbia, South Carolina; Professors William R. Shepherd and David S. Muzzey, of Columbia University; and Professor William K. Boyd, of Duke University. Especial mention should be made of Professor Holland Thompson, of the College of the City of New York, who, in the light of his experience as a writer on southern history, is to a large degree responsible for whatever merit this work may possess. In the reading of the proof the author has had the assistance of Professor William T. Laprade, of Duke University, and Mr. John A. Strausbaugh, of Emory University.

F. B. S.

Edgefield, South Carolina,
September 21, 1925.

CONTENTS

PORTRAITS

MAPS AND GRAPH

THE TILLMAN MOVEMENT IN SOUTH CAROLINA

CHAPTER I

THE BACKGROUND

In order to understand the Tillman Movement in South Carolina it is necessary at the outset to take into account those economic and social changes which made such reforms in the political life of the state as Tillman championed possible and perhaps inevitable. With this purpose in mind, it is necessary, first, to show to what degree the social system of ante-bellum South Carolina was destroyed by forces unloosed by the Civil War and how these new forces made possible the rise to economic and social importance of a class of the white population with little previous influence. This will be followed by an attempt to explain the political changes which made possible an increase of political power on the part of this new class and why this class became dissatisfied with the type of political control existing in the state between 1877 and 1890. Then the way will be open for a detailed narrative, in succeeding chapters, of the rise and the activities of Tillman, the man who took the lead in actually putting this new class in control of political power in South Carolina.

The political control of South Carolina before 1865 was in the hands of an aristocracy of planters to the exclusion of the black and white masses.[1] This was due to the fact that land[2] and slaves[3] were concentrated in the hands of a few, that there were property requirements for office-holding,[4] that political representation was apportioned in favor of the more aristocratic lowlands,[5]

[1] In illustration of this assertion, the author may instance the lives of the sixty-three different South Carolinians who held the offices of governor and United States senator between 1778 and 1865. Only two of this number—George McDuffie and William Smith—appear to have been of humble birth. Perhaps not more than five—David R. Williams, David Johnson, William Harper, Thomas Bennett, and William Gist—belonged to the Baptist and Methodist churches, which were the churches of the white masses. A great majority of the others belonged to the Episcopal Church, which was the church of aristocratic traditions. Eight families—the Rutledges, the Pinckneys, the Calhouns, the Mannings, the Richardsons, the Haynes, the Butlers, and the Pickens—appear more than once on the list, while most of the Charleston office-holding families were inter-related, as were the Mannings with the Richardsons of Clarendon and the Butlers and Pickens of Edgefield with each other and with the Calhouns of Abbeville. See *National Cyclopedia of American Biography* and J. Belton O'Neall, *Bench and Bar of South Carolina.*

[2] In 1795 the average size of landholdings in the state was 310 acres; by 1850, in spite of the great increase in population, this average had risen to 541 acres. *Census of 1860, Agriculture,* p. 222.

[3] Four-fifths of the white population held fewer than ten slaves each in 1860.

[4] Under the constitution of 1790 membership in the legislature was restricted to those possessed of a freehold estate of five hundred acres and ten Negroes, or real estate to the value of £500. *Statutes,* I. 185.

[5] *Statutes,* I. 94-95; William A. Schaper, "Sectionalism and Representation in South Carolina," American Historical Association, *Report,* 1901, gives a full description of the representative system.

and that the white masses, although possessing the right of suffrage after 1808, did not have sufficient education to exercise this right in their own interest.[6]

The Civil War, to a large degree, destroyed the physical basis of society as it had existed in South Carolina prior to that event. Stores were closed; roads were out of repair. Charleston was a "city of ruins, of desolation, of vacant houses, of widowed women, of deserted warehouses and of wharves overgrown with rank weeds."[7] Columbia, where much treasure had been stored, was a wilderness of ruins.[8] Ashley Hall, Middleton Place, Porcher House, and the homes of William Gilmore Simms and Wade Hampton were in ashes.[9] Slaves and Confederate bonds had become worthless, and land had fallen to one-third of its former value.[10] There was much poverty

[6] "The wild Irish", declared Frederick Law Olmstead, "do not differ more from the English gentry than do these rustics from the better class of townspeople." *A Journey in the Seaboard Slave States,* II. 141. "The larger portion of our poorer classes," said a distinguished South Carolinian, "are suffered to while away their existence in a state but one step removed from the Indian of the forest." William Gregg, quoted in H. R. Helper, *The Impending Crisis,* p. 356.

[7] *The Nation* (1865), I. 810-812.

[8] Walter L. Fleming, *A Documentary History of Reconstruction,* I. 17-18.

[9] Sidney Andrews, *The South Since the War,* chs. i, iv.

[10] The value of farm lands had fallen from $10.48 per acre in 1860 to $3.93 per acre in 1870. *Census of 1870, Agriculture,* p. 695. The percentage of land under cultivation during the same period had fallen from 83 to 62 per cent. of the total area. *American Year Book and National Register,* 1870, p. 451.

among those who had formerly been wealthy.[11] From these facts, we conclude that the three traditional elements of the population—the former slaveholders and the white and Negro masses—were forced to begin life anew on a basis nearer equality than had existed since early colonial days.

Under the new order established during Reconstruction the Negro was given opportunity to exercise political power. But this power was destined to be temporary. It was possible only because of the temporary economic exhaustion of the whites, of the determination of the victorious North, acting through the army, to attempt to enforce the principle of universal democracy, of the imprudence of certain white leaders, and of the willingness of the Negro to follow an alien leadership which promised him protection. In spite of the black race's growing superiority in numbers[12] and of its justly praised social and economic advance, at no time during Reconstruction or since has it menaced the economic superiority of the white race. Because the black man has not owned the land, he has been forced to assume the social and economic position of a tenant;[13] because

[11] General M. C. Butler, for example, came out of the War with a loss of seventy slaves and one leg, a debt of $15,000, and with $1.75 in his pocket.

[12] In 1860, 58.6 per cent. of the state's population was colored; in 1870, 58.9 per cent.; in 1880, 60.7 per cent. *The Negro in the United States* (Census Report), p. 463.

[13] Between 1900 and 1920 the number of Negro tenants increased 19,817; whereas the number of Negro farm owners in the same

he has inherited from slavery an attitude of obedience to his former master, he has not been able to resist the determination of his white master to reduce his political power to a minimum. Although he has had some political leaders of ability,[14] he has not had sufficient education[15] and political experience to hold all his leaders to the responsibility of honest government. Once the national government became tired of its somewhat unsatisfactory attempt to uphold Negro government in South Carolina, and once the white minority learned how to nullify the will of the majority without too great an affront to the sentiment of the former enemy states, the collapse of the Reconstruction government was inevitable. In fact, this collapse did come in 1877, when the whites under the leadership of Wade Hampton gained control of the governorship and the legislature. After that date the whites, although ever on guard against the possibility of a return of the Negro to power, could devote their energies to their own questions.

period increased only 3,789. After sixty years of progress, in 1920, only twenty per cent. of the Negro farmers owned the land they tilled. *Fourteenth Census, Agriculture,* p. 276.

[14] Moses, Elliott, Cardozo, and Chamberlain, the principal Republican leaders of Reconstruction, were men of excellent education. *Journal of Negro History,* V. 94-96.

[15] As late as 1920, 28.3 per cent. of the state's Negroes were illiterate as compared with 6.6 per cent. of the whites. *Fourteenth Census, Population,* p. 203.

The break-up of the old social organization and the subsequent failure of the Negro to gain a position of social importance commensurate with his numbers were accompanied by the emergence into importance of a new class of white people, who outdid the ante-bellum aristocracy in the race for the leadership of the state. While the census statistics give us no classifications on which to base judgments as to the relative progress of the two classes of the white population, as they do in distinguishing between the whites and the Negroes, there is evidence to support the assertion that the former slave-holding class has not since 1865 been as successful economically as has a certain portion of the descendants of the non-slave-holding class. In support of this assertion, there are certain indirect evidences of the relative decline of the old families and proof that there has been a relative decline of the more aristocratic coastal area before the more plebeian interior.

The pronounced increase in the number of farms[16] indicates that the great estates of ante-bellum days have been broken into smaller farms. It is a common observation that many of the land-holdings of the older families have passed into the hands of men with new names and traditions.

[16] Between 1860 and 1870 the number of landowners in the state increased from 33,000 to 51,000, while the average size of farms fell from 488 to 223 acres. *Census of 1870, Agriculture*, p. 92.

On account of the economic setback of the War, the demand for wages on the part of their liberated laborers, and the competion of those energetic whites to whom the abolition of slavery made advantageous the practice of personal management of farms, the inheritors of the extravagant practices of the slave system were often unable to manage their estates with profit. Many preferred the low returns from the professions of law and politics to the more plebeian gains of actual farm management. Elements in the white population that had previously been unable to compete with the planter and his slaves used the discomfiture of the planter class to their own advantage. The former overseer, who was experienced in the management of land and Negroes, purchased land from his former employer and went into the business of working Negroes for his own profit. Likewise, the former "poor white," personally experienced in farming, added to the small farm he had inherited from his ancestors tracts of land which the planter sold at a sacrifice. In the towns arose a new class of merchant-farmers, who made small fortunes out of the credit system of financing many farmers, who were forced to borrow after the War. The members of this new class often invested their surplus incomes in agricultural lands. Today, as the wealthiest citizens of many South Carolina communities, they have in some respects taken the places of leadership once held by the ante-bellum planters.[17]

This belief in the economic decay of the aristocracy is reënforced by the fact that the material growth of the more aristocratic lowlands has been less rapid than that of the interior. There has been a rapid growth of manufacturing in the up-country, but not in the lowlands.[18] The utilization, after 1865, of commercial fertilizer has served to turn the sand wastes and exhausted hill lands of the interior into valuable cotton lands. Rice, before the War the chief staple of the lowlands, had, by 1883, declined to one-third of its former value;[19] at present it has almost ceased to be cultivated, with the result that the estates of the rice planters have been converted into hunting preserves of northern capitalists. Charleston, as a commercial center, has, since 1864, suffered a relative decline, due to the fact that the lands near the city have not been adaptable to the

[17] The author's belief in these generalizations concerning the shifting of the titles of land comes from his own observations and those of many South Carolinians familiar with conditions for the past fifty years. He believes that what he says will be confirmed by other South Carolinians who may read this.

[18] The one great industry of Charleston, the mining of phosphates, was, as early as the last decade of the nineteenth century, in decline, due to the competition of the richer deposits of Florida. Reports of Phosphate Commission in *Reports and Resolutions, passim,* 1888-1895.

Between 1872 and 1886 the capital invested in the textile industry of the up-country rose from ten to thirty-two million dollars. Victor S. Clark in *The South in the Building of the Nation,* VI. 283.

[19] A. P. Butler, *Resources of South Carolina,* p. 58.

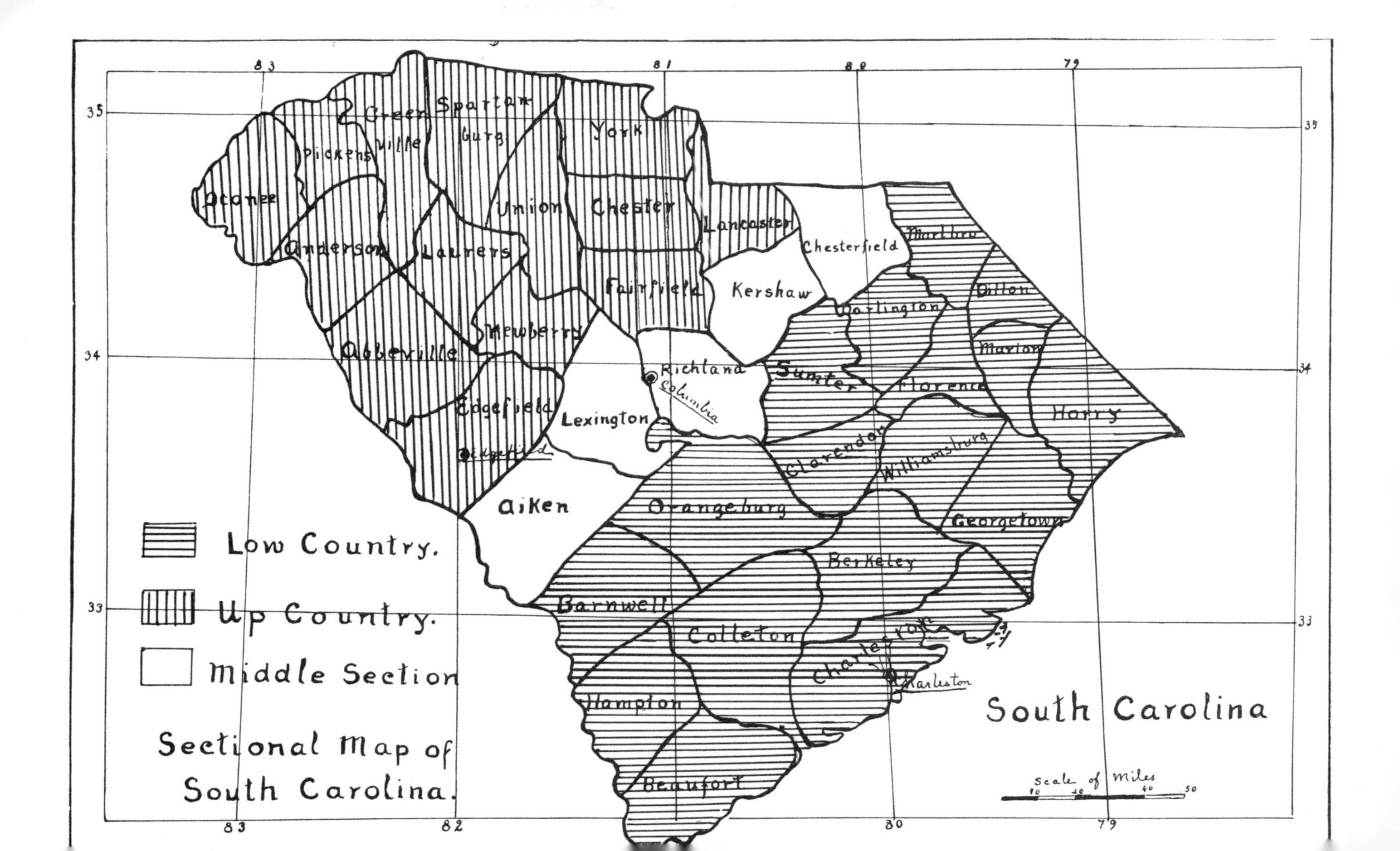

South Carolina
Low Country.
Up Country.
Middle Section
Sectional Map of
South Carolina.
Oconee
Pickens
Greenville
Spartanburg
York
Union
Chester
Lancaster
Chesterfield
Marlboro
Anderson
Laurens
Fairfield
Kershaw
Darlington
Dillon
Newberry
Abbeville
Marion
Richland
Columbia
Sumter
Florence
Horry
Edgefield
Lexington
Clarendon
Williamsburg
Aiken
Orangeburg
Georgetown
Berkeley
Barnwell
Colleton
Charleston
Hampton
Beaufort
Scale of Miles
10
20
40
50

development of manufacturing, owing to the swamps and the absence of water power, and that the industrial centers of the interior of the South have seen fit to use rail routes connected with ports farther north.[20]

The fact that the Civil War changed the economic relations between the white classes did not, however, mean the immediate displacement of the old political leadership after the overthrow of the Reconstruction government. The devotion of the white masses to those who had led them in the War and Reconstruction and the fear that division among the whites might involve a return to Negro rule were sufficient to keep them loyal for a time to the traditional leaders of their race. The result was that Wade Hampton, ranking Confederate officer from South Carolina and member of a notable Richland County family, became by almost universal acclaim the political arbiter of the state.[21]

However, certain political forces were in operation which, taken in connection with the economic changes already described, were destined to make the overthrow of the Hampton régime and

[20] Between 1870 and 1890 the population of Charleston increased by only 1023; there was an actual decline of 50 in the number of whites. Butler, *Resources of South Carolina,* p. 74. The map facing page 10 indicates the sectional divisions of the state.

[21] Hampton became governor and later United States senator. M. C. Butler, member of an office-holding family, received the other senatorship.

the rise of new political leadership inevitable. The political reforms achieved during Reconstruction, the manner in which the victory of 1876 was won, the more or less unsatisfactory manner in which the attempt to deprive the Negro of the suffrage resulted, the failure to solve the problem of agricultural distress, the manner in which the political ambitions of Martin Gary, a popular leader, were frustrated—all these served either to make easier the expression of the opinions of the white masses or to make this element more dissatisfied with political conditions. A discussion of the operation of each of these forces is now in order.

The constitutional conventions of both 1865 and 1868 (the former composed of the leaders of the old régime and the latter of a Negro majority) made possible a wider degree of popular participation in government. The earlier convention reformed the system of legislative representation to the advantage of the up-country and abolished property qualifications for office-holding.[22] The convention of 1868, which was elected by universal manhood suffrage, provided for the election of all officers by universal suffrage and for the reapportionment of legislative representation every ten years on a basis of population and insti-

[22] *Journal of the South Carolina Constitutional Convention of 1865,* pp. 3-4, 41, 139, 186-188.

tuted the principle of universal, free education.[23]

The manner in which the political campaign of 1876 was won was not in every respect satisfactory to those desirous of keeping political power in the hands of traditional conservatives like Hampton. Contrary to the advice of the leaders of the low-country, this campaign was directed by such audacious leaders of popular opinion of the up-country as M. C. Butler, Martin Gary, and George Tillman. The white masses were organized into armed bands known as rifle clubs. These organizations served to intimidate the Negroes to such a degree that a sufficient number were kept away from the polls to insure the election of Wade Hampton as governor. Hampton, by means of his many speeches, did little more than induce a few credulous Negroes to vote for him. Thus the exercise by the white masses of the function of determining who should have political power made easier the transfer to this element of the actual control of politics.[24]

The victory of 1876 was won largely because the white masses cherished an aversion to the political equality of the Negro stronger even than

[23] Ben: Perley Poore, *Constitutions,* II. 1647-1651; *Acts and Joint Resolutions of the General Assembly of the State of South Carolina,* 1870, No. 238.

[24] For a discussion of the campaign of 1876 from this viewpoint see the author's article, "The Election of 1876 in South Carolina", *South Atlantic Quarterly,* October, 1922-January, 1923. The conduct of Ben Tillman and his associates, as told in chapter ii, is an illustration of this attitude.

that of the traditional leaders of southern opinion. Notwithstanding the fact that all sorts of expedients were adopted to lessen the influence of the Negro in politics,[25] the degree of reaction was not yet sufficient to satisfy fully the riotous populace which had won the victory of 1876. However, a full policy of reaction, like that of 1832 and 1865, was prevented by a sense of responsibility toward the Negro, whose suffrage Hampton had sworn to protect,[26] by the fear of the intervention of the national government in the affairs of the state, and by the inertness of the conservative leaders of the low-country. Although the whites were given more than their proportion of the school funds, the principle of universal education was maintained, and the Negroes attended the public schools in larger numbers than the whites. A popular resolution providing for the calling of a constitutional convention, through which the stigma of living under a constitution sanctioned by a Negro majority might be removed, was defeated at each successive session of the legislature. The

[25] Among these measures were: the increase of the dubious Democratic majority in the legislature of 1876 by the expulsion of the Negro delegation from Charleston; the wholesale expulsion of Negroes from public office; so rigid a control of the election machinery that the Republicans regarded a contest of the election of 1878 as useless; the adoption of a system of gerrymandering that concentrated 25,000 of the 30,000 Negro majority in one congressional district; and the publication (1877) of the *Report of the Joint Legislature Committee on Frauds,* which is a bulky indictment of the Reconstruction government. *American Annual Cyclopedia,* articles on South Carolina, 1877-1884.

[26] Charleston *News and Courier,* September 21, 28, 1876.

only plan of suffrage restriction which the legislature could be induced to enact,[27] as a substitute for the necessity of the white man's standing over the polls with his gun, did not entirely exclude the Negro from office. As long as the Hampton influence controlled, black South Carolinians could be seen in both the national and state legislature. The white masses, open and bold in their justification of the suppression of the political aspirations of the Negro, were not satisfied with the halting manner in which their leaders stated their position. When the opportunity came to advance an intelligent justification of South Carolina's solution of the race problem,[28] ample evidence was presented to prove the venality of the Negro government, without a word concerning the tactics used in restoring the whites to power. The reason for this omission was that the conservative leaders regarded any mention of this subject as anathema, evidently being ashamed of the practices to which they felt they had been driven by necessity. The masses desired a leader of sufficient wisdom to

[27] This curious system was known as the Eight Box Law. By its provisions, as many boxes as there were candidates were placed at each polling place; each voter, unassisted, was required to deposit a ballot in each box. If he could not read, there was every chance that he would invalidate his ballots by depositing the ballot in the wrong box. *Acts and Joint Resolutions,* 1882, pp. 1117-1119.

[28] Representative Hemphill in H. A. Herbert, *Why the Solid South,* pp. 85-111.

come forward with a frank justification of what had happened.[29]

In the seventies of the last century the farmers of South Carolina met with economic reverses. The fall of the price of cotton to a point but little above the price of production, the great increase in the number of liens, and the necessity of purchasing farm supplies on credit from usurious merchants at prices twenty to one hundred per cent. above the usual cash prices[30] caused much complaint and a searching about for some remedy. Many, between 1872 and 1875, joined[31] the Na-

[29] An illustration of the attitude of the whites in opposition to the Negro in politics after 1876 comes from the study of the manner in which a majority was returned for George Tillman in contest with Robert Smalls, colored, for a seat in Congress in 1880. The district had been gerrymandered in such a way as to set off Edgefield, a white stronghold, against Beaufort, a black stronghold, with Aiken, Barnwell, and Colleton strung in between. Edgefield, with 3553 whites and 3684 blacks of voting age, gave Tillman the extraordinary vote of 6467, to 1046 for Smalls. The total vote exceeded the voting population by 278. At Edgefield Court House a yelling mob of blacks had been kept from the polls the entire day by red-shirted Democrats armed with pistols and brickbats, with the result that only eleven Republican votes were cast there. At one rural precinct a black leader advanced at the head of a mob intent upon voting. He was captured, beaten, and forced to vote the Democratic ticket, while his frightened following fled. In Aiken, although the census enumerated only 5985 males of voting age, 6447 votes were cast, of which Tillman received two-thirds. The result was that Tillman was declared elected, although he was not allowed to take his seat. *House Miscellaneous Documents,* 47th Congress, 1st Session, No. 20, pp. 36-38; *House Report,* 47th Congress, 1st Session, No. 175, pp. 5, 28, 46.

[30] Charles H. Otkin, *The Ills of the South,* pp. 83-85.

[31] In 1875 there were 342 local granges with a total membership of 10,000 within the state. Solon J. Buck, *The Granger Movement,* pp. 55, 252. The names of these organizations appear in *Rural Carolinian,* August, 1873; January, 1874.

tional Grange of the Patrons of Husbandry, an organization of national extent, which, through its program of coöperative buying and selling and its demand for state regulation of railroads, promised relief. As might have been expected, the Grange was of little practical benefit to the farmers. The attempts at coöperative buying ended in failure due to faulty management, to the impatience of the average farmer with such a slow means of betterment, and to the inability of the farmer-leaders to withstand the temptation of becoming politicians. While Hampton and his successors were most willing to do their best to satisfy the demands of the farmers, they were able to do little. A department of agriculture and the office of railroad commissioner were created, and laws regulating the railroads were passed.[32] But officers of only mediocre ability were put in charge,[33] and the earning power of the railroads was not sufficient to warrant such a radical reduction in rates as would have materially lightened the burden of the complaining farmer. The result was that, after 1875, the Grange rapidly declined in membership, and what was left of it in 1877 joined hands with the conservative Agricultural and Mechanical Society to hold joint annual meetings in various villages of the state for hearing essays on the details

[32] *Acts and Joint Resolutions,* 1879, pp. 72-76; 1882, pp. 791, 843.

[33] Ex-Governor Bonham, for example, was appointed railroad commissioner because he needed financial aid. James Henry Rice, Jr., in the Columbia *State,* August 11, 1923.

of correct farming. "Seldom," said the most zealous promoter of the Grange,[34] "have we [the farmers] acquired any benefit from farmers' associations." But the Grange was not without lasting effect; it taught the South Carolina farmer to believe in the dogma that the state can and should remedy his economic ills. This belief, taken in connection with the fact that in the 1880's the price of staple commodities such as cotton and corn declined both in absolute price per unit of commodity and in the total value of the commodity produced,[35] that the desperate effort of the farmers to establish a cash basis of tenancy ended in failure,[36] and that in two years one million acres of land were forfeited for non-payment of taxes in a state which had only fifteen million acres in cultivation,[37] created an attitude among the farmers making them ready to respond to the call of the agitator most determined in his desire to overthrow the state government then in power.

[34] D. Wyatt Aiken in *News and Courier,* August 10, 1877.

[35] The *News and Courier* in its summary of the economic conditions of the State in its New Year's edition of 1886 said that with an increase acreage in cotton of nearly twenty per cent. the actual money value of the crop was nearly fifteen per cent. less in 1885 than in 1880.

[36] J. E. Walmsley, (MS.) "Causes and Early History of Tillmanism."

[37] Governor Richardson in his annual message of 1887 said: "There were on the forfeited land list at the end of the fiscal year 1886, 954,237 acres. During the present year new forfeitures have been incurred which amount to 100,045, the whole amounting to 1,054,282 acres." *House Journal,* 1887, p. 22.

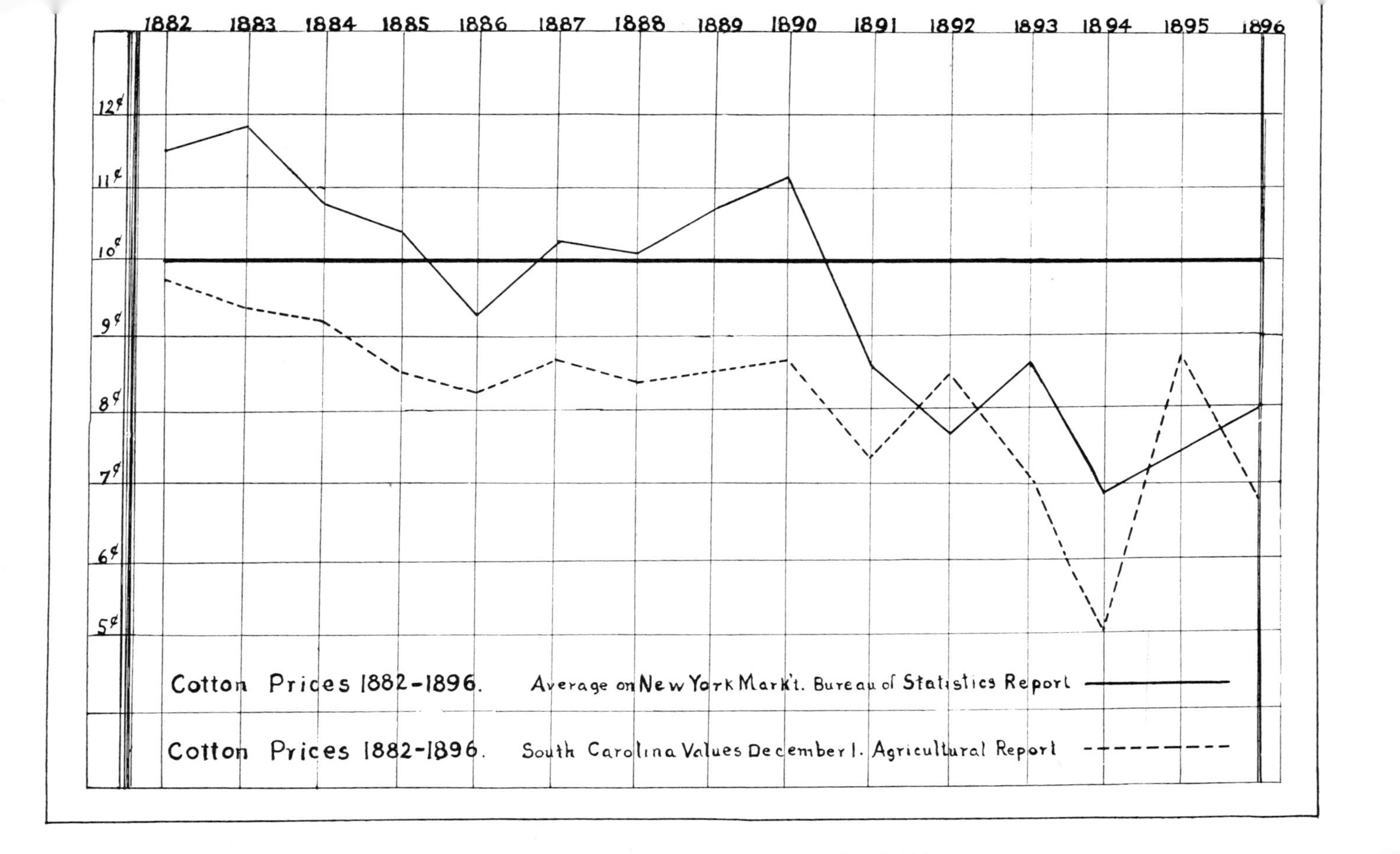
1882
1883
1884
1885
1886
1887
1888
1889
1890
1891
1892
1893
1894
1895
1896
12¢
11¢
10¢
9¢
8¢
7¢
6¢
5¢
Cotton Prices 1882-1896. Average on New York Mark't. Bureau of Statistics Report
Cotton Prices 1882-1896. South Carolina Values December 1. Agricultural Report

Added to the Hampton circle's failure to satisfy the farmers' demands for agricultural betterment, was its failure to satisfy their demands for a wider distribution of the public offices. A fair-minded critic cannot deny that this circle fulfilled in most respects the requirements that are usually expected of public officials. Its members reduced public expenses to an average minimum reached by neither the preceding nor succeeding administration.[38] In the fourteen years of its tenure of power (1877-1890), only one state and an occasional county official were guilty of misappropriation of the public funds, a record far superior to those of the governments of the eight years before and the fourteen years after the passing of the Hampton régime. These men possessed many excellent personal qualities usually associated with aristocratic leadership. Having inherited much of the education and political finesse which distinguished the ante-bellum southern statesmen, they were discreet and capable in politics, even if not brilliant or remarkably constructive. Yet they had an undeniable tendency to appropriate public office for themselves and their friends, to the exclusion of the larger mass of white men. The fact that many men of illustrious ancestry had been reduced to poverty as a result of the War[39] made salaries

[38] See below note, p. 150.

[39] For example, Senators Butler and Hampton and Governors Richardson and Thompson used the salaries they derived from public office to relieve their own financial embarrassment.

attached to public office of more vital importance to them than these salaries had been to their wealthier fathers. Protected by the deep-seated popular aversion to any move that might break the unity of the Democratic party, and acting through the various stages of the convention system for the nomination of public officers, lawyer-politicians, organized in groups around the county court houses and state capitol, regarded the public offices which they held as both a right and a necessity for their existence. In opposition to them there arose groups of farmers, who possessed sufficient influence to make their demands effective because of their rise to economic power since 1865 and who desired office both to effect desired reforms and to enjoy the emoluments of public positions.

The popular feeling against the existing system came to a head under the leadership of General Martin Gary, who, as the most popular citizen of the state except Hampton, desired public office. His distinguished services in the cause of the Confederacy and in the struggle for white supremacy commended him to all white South Carolinians. But his hasty and violent disposition, his bold and profane language, his opposition to the payment of the Reconstruction debts of the state, his championship of a usury law, and his frank statement of the manner in which the victory of 1876 had been won, were characteristics which made him

MARTIN GARY

persona non grata with so moderate and discreet a man as Hampton. In addition, the ambition of Gary to be one of the two South Carolina senators clashed with the ambitions of Hampton and M. C. Butler. Butler, in 1877, defeated him for the first vacancy, and Hampton, in 1879, for the second.[40] The final blow to his ambition was his defeat for the governorship in 1880 by Johnson Hagood, the Hampton candidate. Bitterly disappointed, he returned to his Edgefield home to die within a year.

His attitude towards the dominant political group was expressed before the Edgefield County Democratic Convention of 1880.[41] After telling of his desire "to put into the hands of every honest man a whip to lash the rascals [i.e. the Republicans of the state] naked through the world," he launched into an attack upon the "aristocratic oligarchy," saying:

> Do they want every office? Was one of them ever known to decline an office? Is there not some way to satisfy their greed for office?
>
> Parties are not made for the advancement of individuals and families. The door must be left open for all. . . . The autocratic and aristocratic leaders will be driven to the wall whenever the issue is made up between them and the mass of the people.

[40] His name was not actually presented to the Democratic convention of that year because his friends knew he had no chance of winning.

[41] *News and Courier,* June 3, 1880.

Had Gary lived, it is very likely that he would have led the white masses against the oligarchy. As events happened, the memory of his actions and words lived in the hearts of thousands who felt that he had been wrongly deprived of his reward, and he was a guide to Ben Tillman, the man who actually effected the overthrow of the system Gary attacked.

CHAPTER II

EARLY LIFE OF TILLMAN

The District of Edgefield in 1847, the year in which Benjamin Ryan Tillman was born, had certain characteristics which distinguished it from the ordinary county of interior South Carolina. It was settled a decade before the Revolution by English families from Virginia and a few German, Scotch-Irish, and French immigrants.[1] The introduction of cotton transformed its leading inhabitants from a simple pioneer folk, "who ate from pewter dishes and cut the forests for themselves," into a slave-holding aristocracy of town dwellers devoted to law, politics, and agriculture.[2] In 1814 a weekly newspaper, *The Bee Hive,* was established. A careful observer[3] in 1824 found the village of Edgefield[4] to have three hundred houses, a library of three hundred volumes, a male academy which attracted students from the nearby districts, and a progressive agricultural society.

[1] John A. Chapman, *History of Edgefield,* pp. 6, 8, 28.

[2] In 1790 the whites outnumbered the blacks two to one; in 1820 the blacks were one and one half times as numerous as the whites.

[3] Robert Mills, *Statistics of South Carolina,* p. 525.

[4] The village was incorporated in 1830. *Acts and Joint Resolutions,* 1830, p. 19.

"From 1820 to 1830," according to the historian of the bench and bar of South Carolina,[5] "no interior bar presented abler counsellors than those which appeared in the Edgefield courts." By 1840 the slaveholding gentry of Edgefield—the Butlers, the Pickens, the Bacons, the Brooks, the Carrolls—occupied a prominent position in the political life of the State. In Edgefield lived George McDuffie, a champion of Nullification; A. P. Butler and his avenger, Preston Brooks; F. W. Pickens, the constant advocate of slavery in Congress, who was to become Secession governor; and Louis Wigfall, who as Senator from Texas was in 1861 to win fame as a most radical Secessionist.

Along with this record of distinction should go the fact that Edgefield had a reputation for lawlessness such as is usual in a community that smacks of the frontier. Its citizens were noted for their love of frequent fights, hard drinking, and passionate political feuds.[6] The local reputations of such notable leaders as Brooks and Wigfall were largely based on acts of violence.

Within the limits of Edgefield District, at "Chester," then the family residence of the Tillmans, Benjamin Ryan Tillman[7] was born, August

[5] O'Neall, *Bench and Bar of South Carolina,* p. 279.

[6] This assertion is based on a perusal of the files of the Edgefield *Advertiser,* 1836-1860.

[7] He was named for his father, who was named for Benjamin Ryan (1745-1813), a fellow soldier of Frederick Tillman, the father of the first Benjamin Ryan Tillman. The Tillmans and the Ryans were not related by blood.

11, 1847. Chester was located some fifteen miles south of Edgefield Village and a like distance north of Augusta, Georgia, on the stage road which connected these two towns. The surrounding countryside was and is forested with pine and oak; hills of red clay, between which run deeply embedded brooks, give the landscape a more mountainous appearance than is usual in the middle counties of South Carolina and make the problem of communication so difficult that in our day the builders of railroads and turnpikes have passed to the eastward, leaving this community more isolated than it was in 1847.

There is little in the ancestry of Ben Tillman that calls for special attention. The Tillmans were early English immigrants to Virginia. Roger Tillman, a direct ancestor, held lands in Bristol Parish, Virginia.[8] About 1774 Frederick, Stephen, and Littlebury Tillman, who were brothers, settled in Edgefield District, where they received land grants. In the Revolution, they served under their devoted friend, Captain John Ryan. As was the case of many on the South Carolina frontier, they joined the patriot cause in preference to forced service in the Tory ranks. Frederick, the oldest of the brothers and the grandfather of Ben, possessed considerable lands

[8] *Virginia Magazine of History and Biography,* XVII. 316; XX. 87; XXVIII. 336.

and wrote an excellent hand,[9] but he held no slaves.[10] He married Ann Sebell Miller, who was of German extraction.

Their son, the elder Benjamin Ryan Tillman, inherited the family estate and built Chester. His principal distinction in his community came from the fact that he received stage passengers en route from Augusta to Edgefield. His position as inn-keeper was not one of social distinction, and he seems to have been an unpretentious individual; he was quite thrifty and is described by his noted son as having been "very bright." He left a record of acquittal in 1837 of a charge of murder. He died in 1849, two years after the birth of his youngest son, Ben.[11]

The maternal ancestry of Tillman was more distinguished. His mother's grandfather was Dionysius Oliver, a north Georgia planter of considerable wealth. Oliver's daughter, Martha, came on horseback to Edgefield in 1792 as the bride of Thomas Hancock. Of this marriage was born Sophia Hancock, wife of the first Benjamin Ryan Tillman and mother of Ben.

[9] Records of Land Grants, Office of Secretary of State of South Carolina. 391 acres were granted, August 7, 1787. Folio XII. 577, 1780-1782, Bk. M to Z.

[10] *Census of 1790, Heads of Families, South Carolina,* p. 5.

[11] For the facts of Tillman's family and early life the author depends on a Tillman manuscript, "My Childhood Days", except where other authorities are cited. The Diary of B. R. Tillman, Sr., contains a record of the expense incurred in connection with his trial and acquittal on the charge of murdering a certain Harry.

From this mother came those qualities of distinction which the Tillman brothers inherited. She is described by her son as having been of "commanding figure, five feet, six inches, well proportioned and stately." "She was the strongest woman I ever met," Tillman wrote in after years, "and to her I owe whatever ability I may possess." Handicapped by the misfortunes and dissipations of her sons and by the death of her husband, and sustained only by the devotion of her youngest son and by her own determination, she managed her estate without the aid of an overseer in a manner more efficient than that which characterized many of the neighboring planters. She increased her landholdings from 1800 to 3500 acres and the number of her slaves from fifty to one hundred. Although she was economically able, she did not attempt to rise to social position among the aristocracy of Edgefield village. She was too busy with the affairs of her estate; she possessed neither the ambitions nor the graces of one likely to be successful among the leisurely ladies and gentlemen who composed the social set of Edgefield.[12] Under the care of such a mother, Ben passed his youthful days.

His earliest instruction came from the lips of his mother; his earliest experience came in play with the numerous slaves over whom he was a

[12] For a description of life among the Tillmans, see R. G. Shannonhouse, *Columbia Record,* July 14, 1918.

young lord. At the age of seven he received his first formal instruction from Miss Ann Arthur of New York, a sister of a future president of the United States. She was engaged by the farmers of the community as the private teacher of their children. She taught Ben the rudiments of knowledge and tamed a will more impetuous than that of the usual young master of slaves. Miss Lucy Mills,[13] of Massachusetts, was his second teacher. She rewarded the ability and devotion to duty of the boy by making him her companion in long walks through the near-by woods. Under Eli Sego, described by Tillman as "a typical old field schoolmaster," the youth imbibed additional knowledge. While at school, he formed intimate associations with the other young rustics of the countryside. He took part in their games. Except for evidence of exceptional brightness, he seems to have behaved like a typical country youth.

Although removed, perhaps, as far from the currents of civilization as it was possible to be at that time in middle South Carolina, young Tillman made the most of his scant opportunities for contacts with the culture of the world. He ran

[13] Both Miss Arthur and Miss Mills came South on recommendation of Miss Emma Willard of the Troy (New York) Female Institute, a lady of whom George Tillman had heard while at Harvard. It was not unusual for young northern women to come South as community teachers at a time when the South had no system of rural schools.

eagerly to meet the stage in order that he might get the news from the passengers and secure his copy of a New York weekly newspaper—a veritable mine of information for a young rustic eager to widen his knowledge. Although for months he was without the service of a teacher, and although he was unacquainted with the best books of current literature, he eagerly devoured the limited but excellent library which his brother George had accumulated at their home. He read and reread Ben Jonson, Swift, Bulwer Lytton, Walter Scott, and Shakespeare. His reading was limited only by the capacity of the best, and perhaps the only, library of the neighborhood.

Meanwhile, the lives of mother and son were clouded by the misfortunes of his brothers. Thomas, the eldest, was killed in 1847 at Churubusco.[14] John, the third brother, was "wild, dissipated and handsome." In the absence of the second brother, George, he had tyrannized over Mrs. Tillman "through the sheer weight of his overbearing disposition." Only on George's return was John brought to terms. Said Ben:

> I recall as yesterday a scene I witnessed between the two. When George took him to task, he threatened to kill him [George], and got his pistol. George tore his shirt open, saying, 'Shoot, you damn coward. You are afraid to

[14] His name, along with that of three others of the Tillman name, appears on the monument erected in the Capitol grounds in Columbia in honor of the heroic dead of the Palmetto Regiment.

shoot for no brave man ever threatened a widow and orphans as you have done.' After waiting for a moment with his broad bosom open, George turned and walked up stairs, and John slunk off.

In 1860 John met death at the hands of two brothers, the honor of whose family he had outraged.[15] In the same year Oliver, another brother, was killed in Florida in a quarrel which grew out of a domestic difficulty. Henry, described by his brother as "studious and brilliant," died of fever. James, a brave captain in the regiment of Ellison Capers, died of wounds he received in the Confederate service.

Of George, the sole brother of Ben who survived the Civil War, we must speak in some detail because of his influence on his youngest brother.[16] He early had ambitions to follow the gentlemanly profession of law. After attending the schools of the neighborhood, as was the habit of many of the prominent youths of his day, he entered a northern university. He was a student at Harvard but did not graduate. He completed his legal education in the office of Chancellor Wardlaw, of Edgefield, and was admitted to the bar. During the sessions of 1855 and 1856 he represented his district in the legislature. But his legislative career was cut short by an unfortunate event in the latter year.

[15] John C. and George Mays. For an account of their trial and acquittal, see the Edgefield *Advertiser*, October 10, 1860.

[16] He was twenty-one years Ben's senior.

During a game of faro he killed a mechanic named Henry Christian in a drunken dispute which arose between Tillman and his fellow gamesters.[17] With two rewards offered for his capture,[18] Tillman escaped from the clutches of the law in Edgefield and later fled to Nicaragua, where he became a member of Walker's famous filibustering expedition which was then attempting to subjugate that country. On the failure of Walker's first attempt, Tillman was captured and sent back to the United States. During the winter of 1857-58 he returned to the estate of his mother, a disillusioned adventurer, suffering from a tropical disease, and still a fugitive from justice. For a time he was hid in the upper rooms of the Tillman home. He read all day and only ventured out at night to take long walks with Ben. Finally, on the advice of the family, he surrendered to the sheriff of Edgefield. His trial resulted in conviction of manslaughter. He was sentenced to pay a fine of five hundred dollars and to serve two years in the Edgefield jail.[18a] During his imprisonment he was leniently treated by the friendly jailer and was allowed to devote his time

[17] For an account of the homicide, see the Edgefield *Advertiser,* July 23, 1856. Tillman's reputation for peace had been previously jeopardized by his infliction of a "dangerous pistol wound in the side of Gen. John R. Wever," a prominent citizen of Edgefield. Chapman, *History of Edgefield,* p. 230.

[18] By Governor Adams and the brothers of the slain man. The Edgefield *Advertiser,* November 10, 1856.

[18a] The Edgefield *Advertiser,* November 10, 1858.

to reading. Ben often spent the night with him, and he was allowed to slip away to spend nights at his mother's home. While still in jail, he was allowed to resume the practice of law,[19] and his name appeared in the local paper along with that of two clergymen and the chancellor in recommendation of an atlas,[20] proof that he was even then in high esteem. Yet, even after his term of imprisonment had expired, he was not allowed to appear in court with full powers of attorney, because he scornfully rejected the offer of pardon made by his fellow townsman, Governor Pickens, on the condition that he leave the state.

His next move was enlistment in a state regiment, in which he served with no special distinction from 1862 to 1864. In the latter year he left the army in order that he might take the seat in the state House of Representatives to which he had been elected and in which he might then serve, since his enlistment had given him an automatic pardon. In 1865 he was elected to the state Senate. In the same year he leaped into prominence as a member of the state constitutional convention. During the ten years of Republican control he lived in retirement on the ample estates of his wife at Clark's Hill in the remote western portion of Edgefield County. While his very practical wife busied herself with the management

[19] *Ibid.*, March 13, 1860.
[20] *Ibid.*, April 6, 1859.

of the plantation, George spent his time in adding to the stores of his erratic mind by omnivorous reading. On the return of the whites to power in 1877 he became a member of Congress.

He possessed a unique personality and curious ideas. He was described by Sidney Andrews,[21] who attended the convention of 1865, as "a man of immense frame, very considerable abilities, genial and off-hand. . . . Sitting with great blue eyes that always seem half asleep, he is always on the alert and wide-awake; slouching along in a rolling gait, he is careful and earnest; utterly wanting in powers of oratory or rhetoric, he has made more points of order than any member." His acts of violence, his ungainly and impetuous manners, and his loud and profane speech made him unpopular among the more polite and conservative element of his associates.[22] His strength lay in his appeal to the enfranchised white masses of Edgefield, who gave him their law practice and elected him to office. The one absorbing mission of the man was to attack the "parish system," *i.e.*, the apportionment of legislative representation in such a manner as to give

[21] *The South Since the War,* pp. 81-82.

[22] Chapman in his *History of Edgefield,* has words of praise for everyone except George Tillman. Of him he says (p. 203): "When George D. Tillman came to Edgefield Court House to practice law, he made himself very unpopular in the town and had many enemies. What he was, or is, I know not, for my acquaintance with him is nothing."

the small parishes of the low-country representation out of proportion to their white population. As early as 1856, in a speech of great boldness, he characterized the "parish system as the iron chain which binds 221,734 people, the real men of the State, to the 56,651 *saints* of the parishes." He would have limited the authority of the "oligarchy of five hundred men who are permitted to rule the State with an iron will."[23] In 1865 his attack on the "Chinese conservatism of Charleston" led the gentlemen of the low-country to class him as a "genuine red republican."[24]

The career of George Tillman had a powerful influence upon the developing mind of his youngest brother. As we have already said, George's books and his experiences in travel and in politics were of the greatest benefit to a youth growing to manhood in the backwoods of Edgefield. The misfortunes of George created in the mind of the sensitive boy the impression that the Tillman family had been the victims of injustice at the hands of the village aristocracy. George, he believed, had been driven to homicide because of desperation born of aristocratic snubs and jealousies. The refusal of Governor Pickens to grant his brother an unconditional pardon

[23] *South Carolina Legislative Times,* 33rd Leg., 2nd Session, p. 99.

[24] Andrews, *The South Since the War,* p. 81.

rankled in the heart of Ben.[25] His furious aversion to aristocratic conceits, which he later expressed, may be said to have been produced by the supposed wrongs done to his brother.

In August, 1861, Ben, aged thirteen, was sent by his mother to Bethany Academy to resume his studies. Bethany was located some fifteen miles west of Edgefield and was managed by George Golphin, a graduate of South Carolina College and a competent master of Latin. The efforts of this obscure schoolmaster found expression in the education of Edgefield's most prominent citizens of after years—Tillman, M. C. Butler, and Sheppard. Under his care the progress of Tillman was rapid; the boy was initiated into the mysteries of grammar. His thorough schooling in this subject bore fruit in the conciseness of expression and correctness of diction of one who in 1885 was supposed to be a crude rustic. In 1863 he left school.

The "crazy patriotism"—to use his words in characterizing the Secession movement in Edgefield District—impressed the boy quite differently from those around him. He did not share the enthusiasm of George and the latter's friend, Martin Gary, for the "holiday business" which was to come. The initial movements of the great war—

[25] "The fact", said Ben in "My Childhood Days", "that the proposal of a conditional pardon was made, proved the family's suspicion that there had been a plot to entrap him to kill Christian."

Fort Sumter, etc.—did not make him enthusiastic. In fact, he preferred the pursuit of knowledge to the struggles of war.

He left school in order to help his mother in the management of the family estate. She had fallen in debt to the extent of $20,000, due to the fact that she had endorsed the notes of George, who had speculated unsuccessfully in slaves. Through her business ability and the activity of Ben as collector, the debt was reduced to $5000. The boy, in company with Stan, the old Negro carriage driver, would go to the nearby cotton mill at Graniteville to purchase cloth and to Augusta to market eggs and butter. He proved to be a very practical and efficient agent, although he never failed to use every vacant moment to follow his passion for reading.

In the early winter of 1864, on the advice of his mother, he abandoned the farm in order to return to Golphin's school to be prepared for entering South Carolina College. He lived in the house of his master, being the only student whom war had left. For five months he studied Vergil, becoming well acquainted with that poet. His teacher was too poor to furnish sufficient fare and was unable to provide more satisfactory light than that given by pine torches.

When Tillman left school for the summer vacation in June, 1864, he had received all the formal instruction he was to have. In the trying days following 1865, had South Carolina College been open, neither Tillman nor those of higher social position would have thought of attending it. Yet it may be truly said that, through his own efforts and those of his teacher, he had acquired an education as profound as that of the average graduate of South Carolina College; he only lacked the polish of the college graduate.

He now thought it his duty to join the Confederate army, which at that time contained many younger than this seventeen-year-old youth. He, accordingly, made application to Captain Dixon for enlistment in the latter's company of heavy artillery, then in operation near Charleston. He was duly accepted, as vouched for by enlistment papers now in the possession of the Tillman family. But, a short time after he had left school, on July 10, 1864, he was taken ill with a malady that was destined to incapacitate him for two years, cause the most frightful pain, and result in the loss of one eye. The illness was caused by overstudy, the scantiness of Golphin's fare, the natural weakness of Tillman's constitution, the heat of a pine knot over which he had studied, and an indiscreet swimming venture in cold water.[26] The illness began with intense pain in the left eye caused by an abscess in the socket. By September

[26] That he lacerated his eye on a snag in the brook in which he swam is not true, if we may believe Tillman in "My Childhood Days."

sight had departed from the affected eye. In October he became subject to convulsions caused by an accumulation of pus in the head. In that month Dr. Steiner, an army surgeon, removed his eye and drained off the pus by an incision. How Tillman survived such severe surgery is hardly explainable. Not until two years after his original illness was he well, having lost an eye and the opportunity to serve in the Confederate army, which service would have been a means for later political advancement. Surely the foregoing facts prove that the charge, made after Tillman had become prominent in politics, that he feigned illness in order to evade military service has no real foundation.

On his recovery Ben, then nineteen, was made manager of his mother's estates. After one year of this service at home he went to Florida to take charge of some lands she had purchased in that state. He remained away from Edgefield one year, returning in December, 1868. On his way home he stopped in Elberton, Georgia, where he married Sallie Starke, a member of a family that had previously lived in Fairfield County, South Carolina. The young couple took up their abode in Edgefield County on a four hundred acre estate given to Tillman by his mother, where they resided in a very unpretentious cottage until they moved into the Governor's Mansion many years later. Tillman now began the difficult battle of earning a living in the face of the hard times of Reconstruction. Labor conditions were disordered; his lands were cut with deep gullies and had to be replenished by guano hauled a great distance over muddy roads; and the price of cotton was steadily declining.

In the disorders growing out of the last phase of Republican rule in South Carolina Tillman found his first opportunity for public service. He, along with the white masses of the up-country, was impatient with the slow methods adopted by the responsible white leaders for removing the hated former slave from power. Regardless of law and of the opinion of the outside world, he believed that all means should be used to win in the fight for "civilization and progress in contest with barbarism and the forces which were undermining the very foundations of our commonwealth." "The Creator made the Caucasian of a better clay than he made any of the colored people," was his simple creed and that of thousands less introspective.[27] Acting on this belief, he joined the Sweetwater Saber Club, a company of forty-five men of Meriwether Township, Edgefield County, under the command of A. P.

[27] B. R. Tillman, *The Struggle of 1876,* p. 8. This pamphlet is the author's authority for Tillman's part in Reconstruction when other references are not cited.

Butler.[28] Equipped with uniforms, sabers, and army pistols, Tillman and his colleagues became part of a state-wide revolutionary conspiracy, prepared to use force, if necessary, to rid the state of control by its black majority.

As part of the radical government's plan of protecting itself and its constituency against white force, two companies of Negro militia, commanded by Negro officers, had been organized in Meriwether Township. The numerous parades and drills of the militia were very irritating to the whites. Especially provoking was the conduct of Ned Tennant, the captain of one of the Meriwether companies, who, decorated with a long ostrich plume, paraded himself with scant prudence on his spirited charger. It was inevitable that the white men of Meriwether should make the most of any opportunity that presented itself to reckon with what they regarded as insubordinate conduct on the part of their racial inferiors.

This opportunity came when the whites, provoked by the drumbeats of Tennant's company, which were characteristic of the South Carolina Negro's "mumbo-jumbo" manner of celebrating the fourth of July, resolved, on the morning after the fourth in 1874, to give the Negro captain "a warning that would frighten him or precipitate trouble of some kind so as to bring on a conflict."

[28] A distant kinsman of M. C. Butler and not to be confused with United States Senator A. P. Butler.

The whites fired into the house of Tennant. The latter, frightened, sounded the drum beat for the assembly of his company. Heard for miles around, this served to arouse both races. The news of what had happened was received by Tillman with a "feeling of anxiety, alarm and anger." He immediately sent his wife and the family of his only white tenant to the home of his mother, told his twenty Negro tenants that if "anything happened while he was gone, there would be something to pay for it," and, with two white friends, hurried to the rendezvous of Butler and his company. At noon Butler's command now one hundred strong, marched south to meet the offensive which Tennant was supposed to be preparing. The Negro was asked the meaning "of this unheard of and outrageous assemblage in such a threatening attitude" and was told that if the whites "were not at once assured of his willingness to disperse his negroes" there would be "an attack on him and his crowd." The frightened captain, who in reality had been guilty of no aggressive action, immediately ordered the dispersion of his company. Thus the so-called Ned Tennant Rising ended without a clash or bloodshed.

Yet this occurrence had some of the desired effects. The development of that racial consciousness which was ultimately to result in the subordination of the black race was intensified. The landlords of the neighboring plantations were induced to enter into agreement that they would employ no Negro who belonged to the militia. So effective was this pledge that the only landlord who employed Tennant suffered social ostracism, which led to his suicide.

The next activity of Tillman in the struggle which the rural whites were carrying on against the Negroes was as minority manager of the election in 1874 at Shaw's Mill Precinct. By some "manipulation which nobody ever clearly understood," he confessed, he was able to return a Democratic majority at this precinct in spite of the fact that the registered Negro voters outnumbered the whites by 561 and that the other two managers of election were Negroes. Had the whites been as clever at the other polls, neither Chamberlain nor the black legislative candidates of Edgefield would have been returned. "This was an object lesson," said Tillman, "in the possibilities of what white nerves and brains could accomplish when desperation and necessity prompted action."

Only a few months later Tillman again found opportunity for notable service. While on his way from Augusta in company with his wife, he received news that the home of General M. C. Butler had been burned by incendiaries and that, on "circumstantial evidence and suspicions," warrants charging Tennant and his company with the crime had been issued. Tillman left his wife behind and in great haste hurried to join his company. The house of Tennant was approached for the purpose of arresting him. As he was not found, a *posse* of twenty men was organized to go in the pursuit of him and his comrades. They were found in the woods, and two of their number were wounded by the fire of the *posse*. Frightened by the yells of the wounded, the Negroes scattered. The next day, because a Negro had been bold enough to fire upon a white man, as many as a thousand whites searched the whole countryside for the terrified blacks. So successful was the white terror that no black man, woman, or child remained unhidden. The following day it became known that Tennant's company had with record haste marched to Edgefield village and turned over their arms to the Negro general of militia, who stored them in the court house. Tillman and his colleagues immediately marched to the court house and appropriated the arms for themselves. They could then return to their homes with the assurance that, for the near future at least, there would be no more disturbances in the vicinity of the Sweetwater Saber Club.

In the final phase of the struggle for white supremacy in South Carolina, that is, the campaign of 1876, Ben Tillman did yeoman's service.

Although the time had not arrived when he was to assume a position of leadership, he was among the most tenacious of those who believed that an organized show of force on the part of the whites would be sufficient to relieve the state of the humiliation of black rule. In common with the leaders and white masses of Edgefield, he had no sympathy with the tendency of the more conservative leaders to unite with the reforming Republican Governor, Chamberlain, in order to eliminate from the state the more flagrant forms of corruption. To him, all Republicans bidding for Negro votes looked the same. Chamberlain was no better than Governor Moses;[29] the rule of white skin came first; reform, second.

The opportunity to apply the same methods of terror used in dealing with Ned Tennant came July 4, 1876, when two white youths regarded themselves as insulted because a Negro militia company in company-front parade refused to give way for their passage through the streets of Hamburg, a Negro settlement located opposite Augusta and some twelve miles from Tillman's home. Doc Adams, captain of the company, refused to obey the warrant issued for his arrest for the alleged wrong done to the white youths. The whites, said Tillman, seized this opportunity "to teach the negroes a lesson and to provoke a

[29] Franklin J. Moses, governor of South Carolina from 1872-1874, was regarded as very corrupt.

M. C. BUTLER

riot." M. C. Butler, Martin Gary, and George Tillman, who were the leaders, had even agreed upon the wisdom of letting "the whites demonstrate their superiority by killing as many of them [the Negroes] as possible." This disobedient Negro and his company were driven from their position within a brick building by the fire of the whites. In the melee one white and three Negroes were killed. As many as five Negroes were killed after capture by the whites, who were enraged by the death of one of their number. Tillman was among the most excited of those engaged in the disturbance and among the last to leave the scene.[30]

The response of the Sweetwater Club to the summons to appear for trial at Aiken to answer indictments growing out of the Hamburg riot illustrates how lightly Tillman and his associates regarded the commands of the constituted authority of the state. Armed to a degree unbecoming prisoners at the bar, the troop was received on the outskirts of Aiken by their friends from Edgefield and the entire bar of Aiken, who had volunteered for their defense. At the suggestion of George Tillman, the "Mississippi plan" of uniforming the men in red shirts was resolved upon, in order to terrify the Negroes and answer the

[30] Tillman, *The Struggle of 1876*, pp. 17-28; Simkins, "The Election of 1876 in South Carolina", *South Atlantic Quarterly*, October, 1922-January, 1923.

North for its "flaunting of the bloody shirt in our faces." Ben Tillman and a companion were dispatched to Aiken to get the garments, which were willingly improvised by the women of that place. Standards were made decorated with menacing legends written by the Tillman brothers. Thus equipped, the men entered the courthouse. When the presiding judge ordered them to disarm, his request was refused in violent language. Frightened, he dismissed the indictments.[31]

Tillman, on the promotion of A. P. Butler to the position of colonel of the numerous rifle companies of Edgefield, was elected by his fellows to the captaincy of the Sweetwater Club. Although he was rough in manner and appearance, ungenerous in disposition, and not capable of inspiring intimate personal devotion, he was given this recognition because of his long and zealous service in the interest of white supremacy, his personal integrity, and his commanding manners.

The first opportunity for Captain Tillman to prove his worth in this position of leadership came in the response which he gave to the call for assistance to suppress the so-called Ellenton Riot of September 15, 1876. Colonel Butler had given him notice that one of the two Negroes who had attacked a white woman on the day before was, in company with a group of armed fellows, resisting

[31] Tillman, *The Struggle of 1876,* pp. 30-35; F. W. P. Butler, in the Edgefield *Advertiser,* January 25, 1922.

the efforts of a white *posse* to arrest him. Tillman by noon was under way at the head of a troop of forty men. By late afternoon his command was among the large bands of whites who had surrounded the Negroes in a swamp. A general massacre was prevented only by the timely arrival of United States troops, the commanding officer of whom persuaded both parties to return to their homes. As it was, two whites and twenty-five Negroes were killed.

The rough manner in which Tillman and his colleagues dealt with some of their victims is illustrated by the fate of Simon Coker, a member of the legislature accused of a "very incendiary speech." He was captured by Captain "Nat" Butler, a brother of M. C. Butler, who summarily detailed a member of Tillman's company to effect Coker's execution. The Negro, after prayers and a petition that the key to his corn crib be turned over to his wife, was shot. Tillman defended this act. After enjoying a "substantial meal of barbecued shoat, coffee and corn pone," Tillman returned to his home, leaving the Negroes of Aiken County so thoroughly frightened that they feared to spend the night in their homes.

This was the last active military service in which he took part. The Sweetwater Club became the Edgefield Hussars, an organization principally devoted to the holding of an annual picnic at Lanham's Spring, where beaux and belles gathered for the dance and older folks for barbecued meats and social interchanges.

In the fight to make the Democratic majority in Edgefield County sufficient to insure the election of Hampton, Ben Tillman, as minority manager of election at Landrum's Precinct, did almost perfect service. At 6 A.M. on the day of election he and one of the Negro managers opened the polls. When the second Negro manager appeared, Tillman, in passing upon his right to act, said, "You are too late; but wait until I see what the election law says." The Negro, frightened by the implication of Tillman's words, fled from his post of duty. Another Negro, who attempted to distribute Republican tickets to a waiting crowd of Negroes, likewise fled when Tillman threatened him with death. "Benny Tillman," the Negro later testified, "said they [the whites] had been rulers of South Carolina and intended to rule in the future." The result of the strategy of Tillman was the return of two hundred Democratic to two Republican votes at a precinct which, two years previously, had returned a Republican majority of nearly two hundred.[32]

In the years between 1876 and the time he essayed to be a leader in South Carolina politics, Tillman played a vigorous although not unique

[32] *House Miscellaneous Documents,* 44th Congress, 2nd Session, No. 31, Part 1, Appendix, p. 61.

TILLMAN AS AN AGITATOR

part in the politics of Edgefield County. As a member of the county Democratic executive committee, he advocated the nomination of county officers through the direct primary and full public discussions by the candidates of the issues of the day. He was an ardent admirer of Martin Gary, whose cause he vigorously championed in the Edgefield convention of 1880.[33] He felt keenly the defeat of his chief, although he as yet did not regard himself as the man destined to avenge Gary. In the county convention of 1882 he took a leading part and was elected by that body to the state Democratic convention of that year. At Columbia, however, he gave no indication of the insurgent attitude which he was to assume four years later. Ben Tillman had not as yet found himself. He was still a plain farmer, halting in speech, and more interested in his own farm than in reforming the state.

In 1882, at the age of thirty-five, there had been little in the career of Ben Tillman to indicate that he was soon to play an important rôle in the history of South Carolina. But, once an absorbing issue had taken possession of him, there were hidden in his character many influences that were to give a sagacious turn to his energies. He had sufficient education to make possible the development of ideas and sufficient talent to express these

[33] *News and Courier,* June 3, 1880.

ideas in good English. From his brother George and his family he had assimilated a resentment toward those who were ruling the state. From Martin Gary he had imbibed a militant aversion to the men at that moment in office. In addition, unlike George, he possessed the ability to follow one idea to the end, and, unlike the fiery Gary, he possessed a constructive mind. Whether he would play a part in the state's history depended upon whether he would be sufficiently dominated by an issue to arouse him to action.

CHAPTER III

THE EMERGENCE OF TILLMAN

How Ben Tillman became possessed of a grievance of sufficient weight to send him into public life as a reformer is best told in his own words describing his adventures in farming on his lands:

> I had cleared money up to 1881, and bought land and mules right along. In that year, I ran thirty plows, bought guano, rations, etc., as usual, and the devil tempted me to buy a steam engine and other machinery, amounting to two thousand dollars, all on credit. My motto was, "It takes money to make money, and nothing risk nothing have." To have been entirely free from debt would have made me feel like "a kite without a tail," so I struck out boldly into deep water. Ben Jonson says:
>
> "All men are mortal
> And do have visions."
>
> I had mine and they were rose-hued. Uninterrupted success had made me a fool. I was like the "little wanton boys who swim on bladders"; but I did not know how much of a "bladder" cotton was on land impoverished of vegetable matter in the dry summer.

These investments were followed by a "dreadful drought" and fearful losses which, before he was aware, thrust him in the "Red Sea." An unwise optimism led him to attempt to retrieve his fortune by additional investments. But the result was the purchase of provisions from the merchants at "sickening" prices, continued crop failures in 1883, 1884, and 1885, a pocketbook "like Bill Arp's when an elephant had trod upon it," and the forced sale of much of the land he had purchased.[1]

In other words, Tillman had gone through an experience typical of the American agricultural agitator. He had become absorbed with the idea of making money for himself. Although he had been experienced, industrious,[2] sober, and close-fisted, he had not been able to make a fortune, on account of the disappointments he suffered in common with other farmers of the state. Being somewhat imaginative, he tried the doubtful expedient of gaining a fortune through speculation. He purchased more land and tried farming on a larger scale. He experienced partial failure. Like most American farmers who over-speculate, he was a bad loser. He determined to find a remedy for the evils which he and thousands of other less thoughtful farmer-capitalists like himself experi-

[1] Tillman to Laurence Youmans, November 20, 1887. Youmans' Notebook.

[2] The charge that Tillman was an impractical farmer, made after he had become prominent in public life, is not supported by contemporary observation. A traveler, in 1885, spoke as follows of the manner in which Tillman conducted a farm on a tract of land he had purchased to the north of Edgefield: "Capt. B. R. Tillman is putting in some heavy agricultural strokes about here. This is fine land, and it would be well if there were a hundred such pushing men as Ben Tillman in thirty miles of this place." Edgefield *Chronicle*, April 1, 1885.

enced. The primary weakness of the South Carolina farmer, he believed, lay in the ignorance of the farmer himself. "I discovered," he said, "that not only I know not how to farm, but that very few of us in the hilly parts of Carolina do." He became convinced that it was his duty to go before the public as an advocate of agricultural education.

The first move of Ben Tillman toward the realization of the one idea which was to absorb his attention until he had carried it into concrete achievement; namely, the idea that the farmers of South Carolina needed agricultural education, was the organization in 1884 of the Edgefield Agricultural Club. According to the program which he prepared, an agricultural library was to be established, and conferences for the discussion of the problems of the farm were to be held. But, to the apathetic farmers of Edgefield, this plan made little appeal. The club failed before it began to function.[3] Nevertheless, he was not the man to surrender after a single trial. The following year he revived the organization under the name of the Edgefield County Agricultural Society. Sixty members were recruited, and Tillman was made president. At the monthly meeting addresses from leading farmers were heard. But the society did not prosper. Indifference and dissen-

[3] Tillman MS. "The Origin of Clemson."

sions, originating in the exacting personality of Tillman and his no less exacting demands, reduced the membership one-half.[4]

Yet this experience gave Tillman opportunity to advance himself and his ideas. Without compromise, he gave full expression to his notions of agricultural reform at the June meeting of 1885. Instead of rosy oratory about the greatness of the past and the hopes of the future, such as was then usual in public addresses in South Carolina, he chided the people of the community for failure to attend his meetings in larger numbers and said that to engage in efforts to advance the farmers was a thankless task. He then took a fling at those who cried prosperity in the face of "land butchery" by ignorant farmers and Negroes. "The farmer," he said, "is the creator of wealth. Yet are we enjoying the independence and freedom from care which the tillers of the soil the world over, who own their land, naturally enjoy and which was once the most striking characteristic of our people?"[5]

The reward of this address was a meeting on July 14, which was characterized by a "manifest increase of interest." Tillman was elected one of three delegates to go to Bennettsville, at the expense of the railroad company, as the Edgefield representatives in the joint session of the Agri-

[4] Edgefield *Chronicle*, June 18, 1885.

[5] *Ibid.*, June 24; July 1, 1885.

cultural and Mechanical Society of South Carolina and the State Grange.[6] This election was followed by an invitation from the president of the Agricultural Society to make an address. Accordingly, the first week of August, with a carefully prepared manuscript in his possession, the Edgefield farmer made his way to Bennettsville.

The ninth annual joint session of the two agricultural associations was opened in the Bennettsville courthouse, August 10, 1885, with one hundred fifty-five delegates present. There were no indications that any action outside of the established routine of these meetings was to take place. The court room was sprinkled with sawdust as a protection against farmers noisy in step and careless where they spat tobacco. The rostrum was decorated with festoons of wild olive and ivy, and stalks of corn and cotton lined the aisle. In another room were the agricultural exhibits. The August sun was hot, and the courthouse poorly ventilated. The best minds of South Carolina agriculture read well-chosen but dull (for a hot day) papers on the details of correct farming. Truly, the deliberations of this very respectable meeting dominated by conservative southern gentlemen gave promise of nothing sensational.

But the listless character of the session was broken when Ben Tillman, the inconspicuous

[6] *Ibid.*, July 22, 1885.

Edgefield farmer, arose to deliver his scheduled address. His appearance, his manners, and the contents of his speech were different from that to which South Carolina conventions had been accustomed. Instead of the typical gentleman with long hair and pleasing face, here was one with the appearance of a plain farmer, and with only one eye which, however, flashed. Instead of speaking with fluency and eloquence—qualities which every South Carolinian, even if he possessed no thought, always did manifest if he appeared in public—he read from his manuscript in a high, rasping voice with the hesitancy of a school boy. "As soon as you put a farmer upon his feet he loses fluency," he said in apology for his handicaps. His ideas and words were "like a pair of unbroken colts which never work kindly together." He did not express the usual congratulations for the alleged achievements of the past and the hopes of the future, but uttered many hard truths concerning the past and voiced anxious forebodings. He replaced the usual jokes with much dry humor and wit. In place of the usual Ciceronian prolixity and illustrations from classic history, he spoke with the terseness and caustic coarseness of a Swift and drew illustrations from the soil. Without returning the gracious hospitality of President Duncan with the usual polite words expected of a guest, he had the audacity to use cross words and even to question motives.

He drew a gloomy picture of what he considered to be a decline in the agricultural well-being of the state. At least half of the white population dependent upon the farm for support, he said, were compelled to mortgage their crops in order to get supplies; one-half of the land-owners were merely "hewers of wood and drawers of water. . . . The yoke of the credit system that used to gall no longer frets. The decay of that sturdy independence of character, which once was so marked in our people, is rapid, and the lazy 'descent into hell' is facilitated by the State government, which has encouraged this reliance on others. . . . The people are being hoodwinked by demagogues and lawyers in the pay of finance."

The agricultural department of South Carolina College, which was designed to give the farmers that intelligence which Tillman believed they lacked, was, in his opinion, "just a sop to Cerberus, a bribe to maintain the support of the farmers in the Legislature." Although he did not favor the abolition of that college as a place for the education of lawyers and scholars, he did believe that many of its graduates were "drones and vagabonds," who had been ruined by a political training which unfitted them for usefulness.

In spite of these evils, the manner in which

the farmers and politicians conducted the agricultural and political affairs of the state was grotesque. Six or eight "disreputable politicians," he said, were among the members of the Agricultural Society; yet they should not be expelled by the farmer element, as they might prove strong enough to expel the farmers. With caustic humor, he described the evolution of a farmer member of the legislature into a bad politician:

> He enters the State House a farmer; he emerges from it in one session a politician. He went there to try to do something for the people. After breathing the polluted atmosphere for thirty days, he returns home intent on doing something for himself. The contact with General This and Judge That and Colonel Something Else, who have shaken him by the hand and made much of him, has debauched him. He likes this being a somebody; and his first resolution, offered and passed in his mind, is that he will remain something if he can.

Both the legislature and the Agricultural Society, he warned with sound prophecy, had better reform themselves.

Tillman embodied the constructive portion of his address in a series of resolutions designed to advance the cause of agricultural education. He asked that the Agricultural Society appoint a committee to request the legislature to compel the board of trustees of South Carolina College to execute "in good faith" the Federal laws apportioning funds to that institution for the purposes of agricultural education;[7] that this committee request the legislature to appropriate money for farmers' institutes, to establish agricultural experiment stations, and to provide for the creation of a state board of agriculture composed of farmers nominated by agricultural associations. His hope, expressed in the main part of his address, that the legislature establish "a technical school where the pupils may work and come forth at graduation ready to earn a living," was not included in the resolutions, as he considered the idea inexpedient at that time.

The Tillman address and resolutions had an electrifying effect upon the convention. His speech, said the Columbia *Daily Register*, "was the sensation of the meeting, and almost every sentence was responded to with applause, showing that the farmers were *en rapport* with his scathing irony." However, those who applauded him were only the minority of the delegates and the visiting farmers, who were not members. The officers and a majority of the members were angered by what they considered to be his insulting words. Four of his five resolutions were rejected. Only the one of least importance, that

[7] By the act of 1862, which set aside the proceeds of the sale of western lands "in order to promote the liberal and practical education of the industrial classes" (*Federal Statutes*, II. 850-53), and by the act of 1887, which provided a subsidy of $15,000 to each state that established agricultural experiment stations (*Ibid.*, I. 9).

asking for the establishment of agricultural experiment stations, was adopted. Yet, the fact that he had made his opponents angry had its advantage: it put him before the public eye and made him the leader of those who were discontented with the manner in which the public affairs of the state were conducted; it convinced him and his friends that their wrongs could be redressed only through agricultural organizations other than those before which he spoke.[8]

Although Tillman—still the reticent farmer of the previous months—returned to the retirement of his Edgefield farm and made no immediate attempt to follow up his words by organization, his address created a stir, even in the most conservative circles. The *Greenville News* and several country weeklies were frankly of the opinion that a "new deal" in state politics was necessary. Several newspapers engaged in an acrimonious discussion concerning the nature of the "ring" which Tillman said dominated the state. Even the *News and Courier,* the powerful conservative daily of Charleston, deigned to "investigate" the causes of political dissatisfaction.[9]

In November, Tillman followed what he had said at Bennettsville with the first four of his

[8] For the proceedings of the Bennettsville convention we depend on the accounts of the *News and Courier* and the Columbia *Daily Register,* August 5-8, 1885. The text of the Tillman address is found in Tillman's Scrapbook, No. 1.

[9] *News and Courier,* August 21 to September 1, 1885.

memorable letters to the *News and Courier* on agricultural education. He began these letters by making fun of those who had laughed at his Bennettsville appearance. "I know full well," he said, "that while there was much laughter, it was anything but comedy, and that the farmers behind the railing would have passed the resolutions if they had had a voice in the matter." "I may be a crank," he continued, "—I acknowledge being an enthusiast on the subject of agricultural advance —but if so, I am more than satisfied in the company of those [in other states] who stand for agricultural education." He drew a contrast between the well-appointed Mississippi Agricultural College and the "pitiful, contemptible, so-called agricultural annex to South Carolina College, a classical kite with 'agricultural' written on its tail."[10]

He was not content merely to designate defects and remedies; names were called; hard words were used. The politicians, the state department of agriculture, and the Agricultural Society were victims of his irony. "The farmer standing afar," he said, "sees the money which might go far to revolutionize our benighted and ignorant agriculture divided, frittered and wasted, or boldly appropriated to other uses." The state fair was a place for gambling instead of instruc-

[10] *Ibid.,* November 12, 30; December 2, 7, 1885.

tion. At the meeting of the Agricultural Society he had seen things to cause astonishment and lamentation.

The letters of Captain Tillman served to enhance the reputation he had gained at Bennettsville. They were unlike anything which his generation of South Carolinians had read. The discriminating asked themselves, who was this abusive farmer who expressed himself in such excellent English, was master of a terse and unique style, had read Don Quixote, and knew something of Greek and Latin and of the history of industrial education? The fact that he questioned motives and called names involved him in lengthy and bitter controversies with certain public officials. These personalities served to arouse curiosity about him on the part of a majority of South Carolinians, who had become more interested in personalities than in abstractions and in a constructive program of agricultural reform. Although Tillman's language was violent, there was sufficient moderation in his ideas and his charges to attract the confidence of a state so fundamentally conservative as South Carolina. There was no attack upon the principle of private property, nor was there any appeal to the Negro, or words in the Negro's behalf. He spoke as a conservative landowner bent upon effecting certain reforms which he believed would benefit his class. While he charged that the officeholders of the state had been negligent, he was careful not to charge them with dishonesty.

The only immediate recognition which the men in control of affairs gave him came from the board of trustees of South Carolina College. That body recommended, in its annual report to the legislature, that the work of the agricultural annex to the college be made more practical by the establishment of agricultural experiment stations.[11] But the legislature of 1885, angered by the dictatorial manner of the up-start farmer, was in no humor to accept this suggestion.[12]

Tillman, aroused by the retorts of his antagonists, and deeply convinced that it was his duty to put his whole energy into the fight for a more effective means of agricultural education than that afforded by the state college, followed up the suggestion, made in one of his letters, that those farmers of his way of thinking should organize and make an active attempt to convince the farmers of the necessity of an agricultural convention. "The farmers," he cried,[13] "have acted like cowards and idiots in the past; whether or not they are going to run the State in the future is for them to say." He made many addresses through-

[11] *Reports and Resolutions*, 1885, I. 203.

[12] *News and Courier*, December 15, 1885. For Tillman's comments, *Ibid.*, December 21, 1885.

[13] *News and Courier*, January 8, 1886.

out the state and organized numerous county and township agricultural clubs. He was given the derisive titles of "Farmer Tillman" and "the agricultural Moses." He was quick to turn these and more abusive epithets to his own advantage, knowing the benefit of picturesque derision and that abuse is an excellent asset to a rising politician. Every newspaper had something to say about him—a few gave praise; some knew not what to say; many condemned him.[14] "Mr. Tillman," said an observer commenting upon the effects of his agitations,[15] "has no conception of his popularity among a certain class of political farmers. He may be elected Governor, who knows?"

His next move was an address written by him, signed by him and ninety-two other farmers, and published in the newspapers of the state, calling the farmers to meet in convention at Columbia, April 29, 1886. The farmers, the address maintained, constituted seventy-six per cent. of the population of the state and "may justly claim that they constitute the State, although they do not govern." Notwithstanding the fact that the legislature of 1885 had many farmers in its

[14] This statement is based upon numerous opinions of the press of the state published in the Columbia *Daily Register,* January 1 to April 9, 1886.

[15] The Lancaster correspondent of the *News and Courier,* March 5, 1886.

membership,[16] this body was caustically censured for alleged neglect of agricultural interests. The author of the address was dissatisfied with the type of agricultural consciousness which the legislature represented. He would have class-conscious and aggressive farmers—a type new to the decade; the farmers, who, as he expressed it, had been content to be mere taxpayers and to occupy the position of the "mudsill" of society, should organize themselves in such a manner as to make possible their control of the political affairs of the state.

In response to his suggestion, county conventions representing community agricultural clubs were held on April 5. The Edgefield assembly praised Tillman for his "sterling qualities" and for his "intrepid bearing and wise counsel in 1876"; his movement was endorsed, and he was elected leader of a delegation to go to Columbia.[17]

At noon of the appointed day, the Farmers' Convention assembled in the state Agricultural Building with three hundred delegates present, representing all but five of the thirty-five counties of the state. This excellent attendance was a proof of the far-reaching effect of Tillman's agitations. Among this three hundred, only twelve

[16] In 1885 seventy-one per cent. of the members of the House of Representatives were farmers, while the Senate was composed of eleven farmers, fourteen "planters", and ten lawyers.

[17] *News and Courier,* April 7, 8, 1886.

had been members of the last legislature; only two or three were lawyers; five were editors; twelve were physicians; the remainder were "simon-pure" farmers, tasting for the first time the delights of a political gathering. "It was," said N. G. Gonzales, a hostile observer,[18] "a convention of intelligent South Carolina farmers with a few black sheep [*i.e.,* men with alleged Republican affiliations] among them." The great majority, like their leader, were property holders anxious for some redress of their agricultural grievances, without any desire for radical social reform.

The personal appearance of Tillman, as he arose from behind the simple pine table to call the convention to order, did not make a favorable impression upon Gonzales. "He is of middle height, swarthy complexion and spare built," said this reporter. "His single eye sparkles and snaps when he begins to 'whoop up things,' but his face in repose is neither handsome nor attractive. It certainly gives no idea of the brain power which it conceals." He wore a dark blue coat, black pants, and a black silk handkerchief, which "rode up" and concealed a narrow standing collar. His appearance revealed him as he really was, a farmer attempting to present himself to the public with some show of grace.

[18] *News and Courier,* April 30, 1886.

But the fact that behind this rude exterior there was a live personality was apparent as soon as he began to read his address. He spoke with great fire in a high and rasping voice. He made his points of emphasis effective by cunning halts and gestures. He drew illustrations from Carlyle and *Tristram Shandy* and expressed himself in a clever mixture of the choicest English and the slang of the countryside, as though some eighteenth century pamphleteer had emerged from a South Carolina farm. He eloquently glorified his title of "Moses" and hurled caustic bits of sarcasm at those who had attacked him and "the old lady" (the Democratic party). He laughed at those newspapers which had gotten "off the fence and had either become silent, or blatant advocates of the farmer and his rights." He expressed an unabashed opinion of the office-seekers. "The little greedy men, the office-seekers and their satellites, judging me by their own mean standards, have cried, 'He only wants office'." It was a pity that in so short a time purity in the state government had been succeeded by "political leprosy." In making explicit denial that he would yield to the temptation to become a candidate for governor, he quaintly said: "I have told the devil to get behind me. I commenced this fight pure and honest, and only a farmer. I will end it as I began, and for a reward I only ask your good opinion and confidence." Yet he repudiated the advice of those who would have the farmers beware of the dangers of politics, crying:

> Say, you men who own the soil of South Carolina, . . . how do you like this wet nursing, this patronizing, this assumption of superiority, this insufferable insolence? . . . Let us agree on what we consider just for us and for the State and see to it that in the next Democratic primaries men are chosen who will loyally carry out our wishes.

The convention, both in feeling and action, agreed with Tillman's address. A motion that Governor Thompson be invited to address the assemblage was opposed from the floor by a delegate, who said that "the work of the convention should not be overshadowed by one who has recommended wrongful appropriations." Although these words were interpreted by a minority as insulting to the Governor, the assembly approved of them to the extent of waiting until the next day to invite the Chief Executive. Only twenty-seven votes could be mustered in opposition to Tillman's resolutions, all of which were adopted. They provided for a convention of farmers, to be known as the Farmers' Association, to meet each November; for a permanent executive committee composed of one member from each county, of which Tillman was made chairman; and for a committee, of which Tillman likewise was made chairman, to appear before the legislature to advocate certain reforms. The principal reforms advocated were a separate agricultural annex to the state college and a tax on fertilizer. The other reforms advocated were a state board of agriculture elected by a farmers' convention, the repeal of the lien law through which so much agricultural property had become mortgaged, the establishment of an industrial college for young women, and the calling of a convention to make a new constitution.[19]

The convention had been a great success. A program, far more conservative than the previous utterances of Tillman seemed to indicate, had been adopted. A numerous group representative of the landowners of the state had become acquainted with each other and with their chief and had created a permanent organization through which they planned to change the policies of the state government. Furthermore, the convention was a personal triumph for Tillman. His speech was delivered in such a manner as to delight his auditors and to give him self-confidence. His bold assumption of single-handed leadership was rewarded by the fact that his ideas were made those of the majority. He had taken the first step towards achieving that position of dictatorship in the political affairs of South Carolina which was in keeping with his nature.

[19] For the proceedings of this convention see the *News and Courier* and Columbia *Daily Register*, April 29-30, 1886, and Notebook of Laurence Youmans (MS.).

CHAPTER IV

THE FARMERS IN POLITICS

The immediate objective of the farmers, now that they were organized, was to capture the machinery of the Democratic party and thereby insure the election in 1886 of a governor and a legislature favorable to their program. But, since most of them were new to politics, they were slow to act. Tillman, having eschewed political ambition for himself, was uncertain as to which candidate for governor he would support. Of the ten men suggested as possibilities—among whom were both George and Ben Tillman—John C. Sheppard and John Peter Richardson loomed largest. Sheppard had had a notable career in the legislature, had been elected lieutenant governor, and had become governor in 1886 on the resignation of Governor Thompson. He was eloquent, very cautious, and, for the most part, a self-made man. Richardson possessed qualities which commended him to the element in South Carolina not anxious for change. He came from a family which had already given the state four governors; he enjoyed the support of those in sympathy with his ambition to redeem the family fortune by resorting to politics. Possessed of good manners and a moderate degree of eloquence, he was of the type not likely to disturb the political peace.

Not having a candidate who fitted into his own ideas of political reform, Tillman preferred Sheppard to Richardson. Sheppard was a native of Edgefield, a former schoolmate of Tillman, and was endorsed for governor by the same county convention that elected Tillman as the leader of its delegation to the state Democratic convention, which was to meet in August for the purpose of nominating a governor. In the face of the inability of the farmers to capture a majority of the county delegates, Sheppard appeared to be the most available man. Tillman hoped that he could be induced to endorse the farmers' program, in view of the fact that he had taken no part in the political controversies of the past year. On the eve of the convention, however, any expectation that he would endorse the Tillman program was destroyed by the fact that he expressed himself as out of sympathy with this plan.[1]

In spite of the failure to make a satisfactory choice of a candidate for governor, the members of the Farmers' Movement showed great political activity. Farmer Tillman, while not engaged in

[1] *News and Courier,* September 1, 1886.

the press of farm work, continued his letters to the *News and Courier,* defending with characteristic vigor the work of the Farmers' Convention and answering many personal attacks. The farmers of South Carolina, in the opinion of an outside observer,[2] had "come out of the shades of private life" to capture as many county conventions as possible. The result was that, when the state convention assembled, the farmers lacked a majority by only thirty votes.

At a secret caucus of Tillman delegates, held on the eve of the convention, an attempt to endorse Sheppard failed. As no other candidate of an importance sufficient to make his election likely was found to be in favor of the Tillman program, the conference instructed its members to vote as they pleased. Had Sheppard been willing to accept the Tillman program, he would probably have received the nomination, as Dawson, the leader of the Charleston delegation, and other independents outside of the farmer bloc were prepared to vote for him. As the situation developed, Tillman, in seconding Sheppard's nomination, said that he did so as a private citizen and not as a representative of the farmers. The result was that the farmers' votes were scattered, and Richardson won the nomination by a majority of thirteen.

[2] The Augusta *Chronicle,* May 14, 1886.

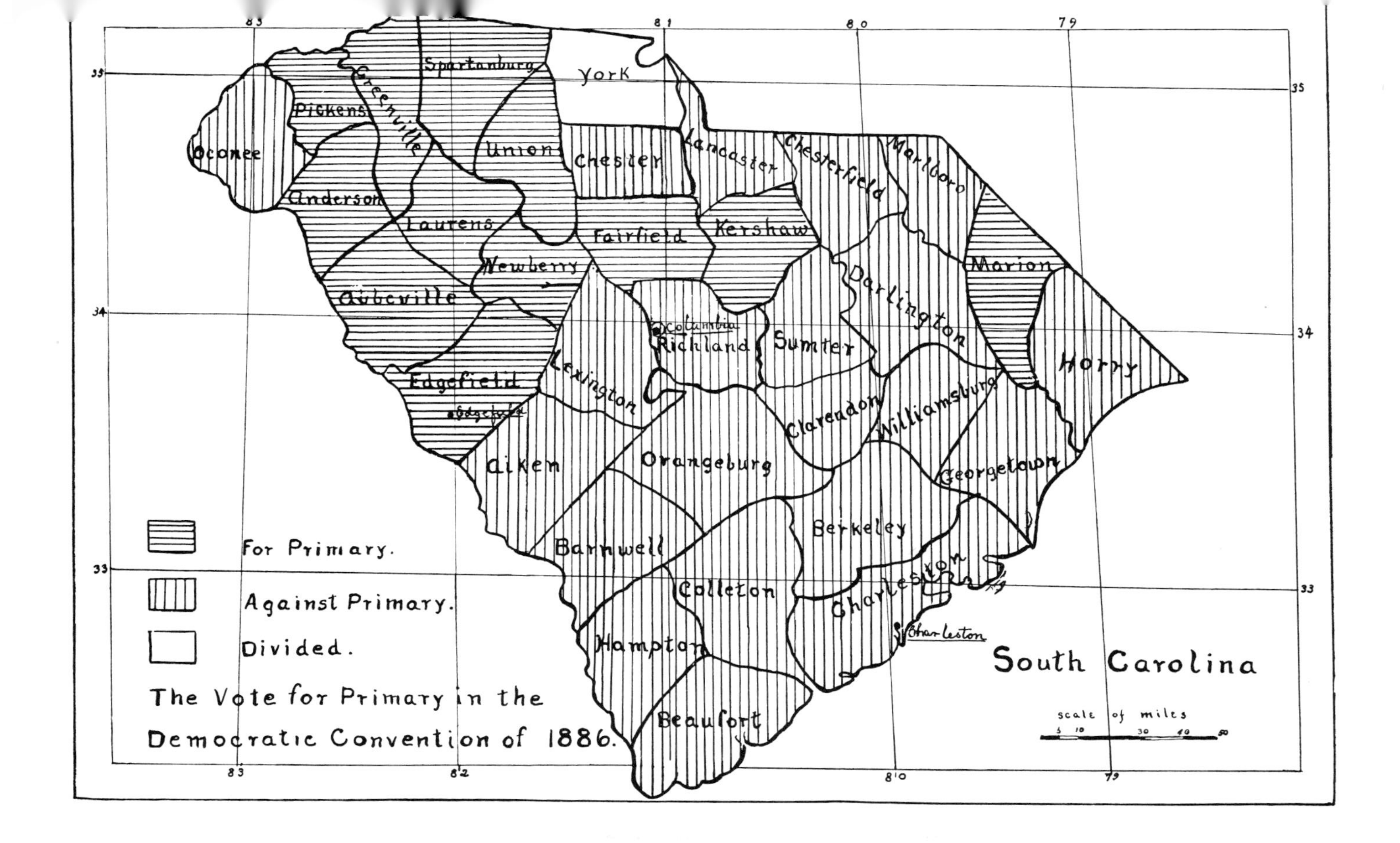

The Vote for Primary in the Democratic Convention of 1886.

The farmers likewise failed in their efforts to secure the party's endorsement of portions of their program. The convention voted down proposals for a constitutional convention, for the apportionment of representation in future Democratic conventions according to white population, and for the nomination of state officials by direct primary.[3]

Between the time of this convention and the scheduled Farmers' Convention of November, Tillman kept himself before the public eye by engaging in a wordy battle with a clerk of the agricultural commission. He said that that department wasted $25,000 annually, and yet he had been told that there was no waste and extravagance, "no Democratic imbecility." In reply, the clerk accused him of "swaggering bravado" and of lying about the department. Tillman, in answering, took the position of a proud landowner contemptible of the mere clerk and "mercenary scribbler." He lamented the temptation "to emulate his [the clerk's] dirty language" and fight a duel with him, or go to Columbia to strike "one so contemptible that if I killed him it would be murder; if he killed me it would be justifiable homicide."[4] This illustrates the intense serious-

[3] For the proceedings of this convention, see *News and Courier,* August 4-7, 1886.

[4] That is, it was a greater crime for a great man to kill a pigmy than *vice versa. News and Courier,* September 22, 28; October 7, 1886.

ness of the man, the limit to which he would go in order to destroy those who stood in his way.

The second Farmers' Convention met as scheduled in November. However, it lacked the enthusiasm of the first meeting. There were fewer present, due to the rival attraction of the state fair; the hall was cold. Tillman, as chairman of the executive committee, opened the meeting with another address. He warned his enemies not to believe that the movement was a failure, for the farmers had failed to carry the August convention only because of suspicions against him. A large portion of the coming legislature had been won, and the farmers were being slowly educated to look after their own affairs. He believed that his aims could be achieved if the farmers would "guard against the Board of Agriculture's and the proposed Agricultural College's being made asylums for broken down politicians and superannuated Bourbon aristocrats, who are thoroughly incompetent, but are ready to put in their claims for every position of honor and profit." Nevertheless, he did not minimize the difficulties which stood in his way. It was necessary to elevate a people falling deeper and deeper each year into a "slough of despair" caused by "the greatest of all taxes, ignorance. Yet to combat the ignorance, the prejudices, the apathy and the egotism of our agricultural population is a well-nigh hopeless task and some of our pets will squeal when the public teat is slipped from between their mouths."

While there can be no doubt that less enthusiasm was manifested at this meeting than at the one of the previous spring, the principal work for which it was called was effected. Tillman and two others were appointed members of the committee to go before the legislature. He and nine others were recommended for election to the new agricultural board, which the legislature was asked to create.[5]

At the opening of the new legislature, in December, the representatives of the Farmers' Convention were much in evidence. Representatives J. L. M. Irby, of Laurens, and J. E. Tindal, of Clarendon, and Senators Jasper Talbert, of Edgefield, and J. A. Sligh, of Newberry, were there as important champions of the agricultural program. Tillman and the two other members of the legislative committee did active service in the lobby.[6] Yet neither the outgoing nor the incoming Governor encouraged their activities. Sheppard praised the work of the agricultural annex of the state college and the department of agriculture, but he did not commit himself on the question of the

[5] Tillman Scrapbook, No. 1; Augusta *Chronicle,* November 10-12, 1886.

[6] *House Journal,* 1886, p. 9; *News and Courier,* November 24, 1886.

constitutional convention.[7] Richardson contented himself with a eulogy of South Carolina as "the most advanced and progressive of the States."[8]

Early in the session bills providing for many of the Tillman projects were introduced. Salaries of public servants were to be reduced, the lien law repealed, the agricultural department reorganized, a constitutional convention called, the royalty charged the phosphate miners for the exploitation of the state's rights in that commodity increased, and a separate agricultural college established.[9] The attempt to decrease expenses through the reduction of salaries was deemed unwise, in view of the fact that public salaries were already quite small. The effort to repeal the lien law was defeated by a large vote.[10] The bill for the reorganization of the agricultural department passed the House, but was defeated by the Senate because that body resented "Tillman dictation."[11] The project for the calling of a constitutional convention was defeated, because this agitation was interpreted as "but an evidence of the fever and ferment in the public mind, which is in itself the best reason why the convention should not be

[7] *House Journal,* 1886, pp. 37-39.

[8] *Ibid.,* 1886, pp. 39, 50, 52.

[9] *Ibid.,* 1886, pp. 114-120; The *News and Courier,* December 4, 1886, published the text of the college bill.

[10] *House Journal,* 1886, p. 187.

[11] N. G. Gonzales in *News and Courier,* December 22, 1886; *Senate Journal,* 1886, p. 311.

held."[12] The phosphate measure was postponed because no way could be found to abrogate the contract existing between the state and the mining companies. The agricultural college bill was abandoned in favor of Tindal's bill for the establishment of agricultural experiment stations and for the appointment of a commission to investigate the desirability of a college. While both measures passed the House, only the bill for the experiment stations received the approval of the Senate.[13] Thus, only one constructive measure designed for the benefit of the farmers became law, and this was a radical modification of the farmers' notions as to how agricultural education should be obtained.[13a]

The reason why the farmers' program did not receive the support of the legislature was that a majority resented the blustering and dictatorial manner in which Tillman went about the achievement of his aims. There were no other reasons why a body of moderate men, dependent on an agricultural constituency for election, should reject a program of reform so moderate as that

[12] From a Charleston representative's speech. *News and Courier,* December 18, 1886.

[13] *Senate Journal,* 1886, p. 383.

[13a] The experiment stations did very effective work under the able direction of J. M. McBryde, president of South Carolina College and its professor of botany—South Carolina Experiment Station, *Report,* 1888, pp. 6-10. When political changes deprived McBryde of adequate opportunity to exercise his talents in South Carolina, he went to Virginia, where he had success as organizer of the polytechnic institute of that state.

proposed by the Farmers' Convention. Tillman was quick to understand. But, instead of retiring to private life in order that more moderate leaders might achieve those reforms which he desired, or instead of entering the legislature[14] in order that he might through personal contact convince a majority of his good intentions, he preferred to continue the difficult rôle of public censor from his front porch, without checking in any degree the denunciatory character of his writings.

Accordingly, two weeks[15] after the adjournment of the legislature, he caustically arraigned the Senate and its leader, Laurence Youmans, for its defeat of his measures. The "oligarchy of lawyers," he said, had taken advantage of "the fuss kicked up" by Youmans and the other farmers of the body over Tillman's personality "to plant a sly dagger in the measures which he proposes." "My animus," he continued, "was not against the agricultural solons for whom I feel pity and contempt, but against the lawyers who should have deferred to the wishes of the farmers met twice in convention." "If the farmers who sent these men to the Legislature," he concluded, "have any self-respect; if they have any manhood; if they are not the dogs they are taken for, they will see to it that these men are properly rewarded.

[14] He was offered a seat, which he politely declined.
[15] In *News and Courier,* January 6, 1887.

If we cannot reorganize the Agricultural Department, we can reorganize the Senate."[16]

These hot words were followed by the acceptance by Tillman of a challenge from Youmans to meet him in joint debate at Barnwell, the home of Youmans. So successful was Tillman's rude and pointed manner of speech that for two hours the excited audience refused to allow Youmans to speak above its cries.[17] Having proved to be as effective in public speech as in the use of the pen, Tillman followed his Barnwell address by many others throughout the state.

In the meantime, official and patriotic South Carolina held at Spartanburg a so-called Inter-State Encampment of Farmers, designed to give the farmers instruction and entertainment. Tillman, refusing to attend as a guest, was severe in his criticisms. The encampment, he said, was only "a rendezvous of all men who shut their eyes to the present and worship the past," and a means by which "pleasure-seekers were enticed from their homes by a fanfaronade." Its promoters—Bourbons, doctors, lawyers, and politicians—lacked the intelligence necessary to manage a farmers' fair.[18]

[16] Youmans' answer, *News and Courier,* March 9, 1887; Tillman's reply. *Ibid.,* March 19, 1887.

[17] *Ibid.,* November 1, 1887.

[18] *Ibid.,* August 6, 1887.

These letters and addresses were followed by the third regular session of the Farmers' Association in November. This meeting was of hardly more than routine importance, as little could be expected from the hold-over legislature of 1887. A vain attempt was made on the part of a considerable faction opposed to Tillman to have the convention declare itself as disapproving of his attacks on the officials of the state and of a separate agricultural college. While Tillman took no prominent part in the proceedings and did not even reply to the attacks of his opponents, he remained in control of the assemblage.[19]

Notwithstanding the somewhat colorless character of the Farmers' Convention, the session of the legislature of 1887 was the scene of a long battle between the friends and opponents of the farmers' program. Senator Talbert made a strenuous effort to have the board of agriculture reformed according to the farmers' ideas, without success. The majority contented itself with enlarging the board and electing as the new members men who had not received the endorsement of the Farmers' Convention.[20] A resolution for the calling of an election in which the people might pass upon the question of a constitutional convention was defeated by the Senate and later passed by

[19] Columbia *Daily Register,* December 2-3, 1887.

[20] *Senate Journal,* 1887, p. 181; *House Journal,* 1887, p. 329; *Acts and Joint Resolutions,* 1887, p. 802.

that body under the pressure of public opinion, but it failed to receive the necessary two-thirds vote of the House.[21] The most bitter struggle of the session was over the bill for the apportionment of representation in the legislature according to the census of 1880, as the constitution required. This measure aroused the rivalry between the up-country and the low-country, as it involved a gain of representation for the former section at the expense of the latter.[22] It failed because of the opposition of the Senate.[22a]

The outstanding accomplishment of the session was the adoption of Governor Richardson's recommendation that South Carolina College be renamed the University of South Carolina and that a college of mechanical arts and agriculture be created as part of this institution. The Tillman leaders, in the face of galleries in favor of the new arrangement, made vain attempts to have the agricultural college excluded from the new order. It was quite evident that the purpose of the act making into a "university" a college which had only 192 students, and which was destined to have fewer, was an attempt to frustrate the advo-

[21] *House Journal,* 1887, p. 331.

[22] Charleston would have lost four representatives and Hampton and Richland one each, to the gain of the low-country county of Beaufort and the counties above Richland.

[22a] *House Journal,* 1887, p. 189; *Senate Journal,* 1887, p. 206; *News and Courier,* December 10, 14, 1887.

cates of the separate college.[23] The only victory which the farmers won at this session was of a negative nature: they prevented the reassignment of the state's phosphate franchises to five mining companies for the small royalty of two dollars on each ton mined.[24]

Tillman was both exasperated and disappointed with the legislature's second failure to enact his program and so expressed himself in his famous "Farewell Letter" to the *News and Courier.*[25] The "green Legislature," which had desired to effect reform, had been "debauched" by the Columbia Club, whose "free liquors and free entertainment has so *won* the good-natured farmers that they would not say nay to demands of the clubmen." Such "malleable and complacent material" should be retired to private life. Concerning the new university, he spoke words of warning: "Let its friends crow lustily over the great victory they have won," but the poor farmers, who can not afford to send their sons to this institution, will show these "lordly planters" that they can get what they ask. Because he was not elected to the board of agriculture, he ironically spoke of his words "as the mutterings of a ghost, the howl of a disappointed office-seeker"

[23] *House Journal,* 1887, p. 220; *Senate Journal,* 1887, p. 194; E. L. Green, *A History of the University of South Carolina,* p. 438.

[24] *News and Courier,* December 15, 1887.

[25] *Ibid.,* January 6, 1888.

who would not have the pleasure of "a junketing tour" with the "Bee-man from Spartanburg, the Sheep-man from Chester and the Jersey-man from Anderson" to inspect the phosphate deposits. He bade Charleston, whose representatives had opposed the re-apportionment of representation and the constitutional convention, not to risk the possibility of a return of the Negro to political power in the event that there was a division among the whites. The city had better lose some of her representation than tolerate the refusal of "our imbecile statesmen" to "draw the fangs of the negro monster" by calling a constitutional convention. He expressed himself as confident that he had on his side the numbers necessary for the success of his plans, but that he only lacked an organization. "Although," he warned, "the Ring newspapers take up the rôle of jackals in declaring that Captain Tillman is a dead duck, but unless I am mistaken the farmers will be on hand 'to make Rome howl'."

Yet he now went into temporary retirement, placing the management of the Farmers' Association in the hands of others. He rightly felt that the failure of the legislature to enact his program had been due to his personality. He likewise believed that the welfare of his family demanded that he give more attention to his sorely neglected farm. So, with much praise from an opponent for his "honesty of purpose, his energy of expression and his intelligent work in arousing the farmers of the State to better methods of farming,"[26] he resolved to keep his peace on his farm. But this retirement was not irrevocable; he was by nature too restless, and he felt too deeply the justice of his program, not to be ready to become active again when more fortunate circumstances should arise. Or, as he expressed it: "He had not lagged superfluous upon the stage; he could with grace permit himself to come upon the stage again."

Scarcely more than three months after the "Farewell Letter," an opportunity "to come upon the stage again" presented itself. Thomas G. Clemson, a son-in-law of John C. Calhoun, died April 6, 1888, leaving Fort Hill, the Calhoun estate of 814 acres, and a cash endowment of $80,000 to be used by the state for the establishment of a separate agricultural college. Clemson, a graduate of the Paris School of Mines and a pioneer in the advocacy of scientific agricultural education in South Carolina,[27] had been induced by Tillman and two others interested in this subject to leave his property for the establishment of the college. By a provision of Clemson's will, Tillman and six others were to become life trus-

[26] See Dawson's editorial, *News and Courier,* January 26, 1888.

[27] See, for example, his address in Agricultural and Mechanical Society of South Carolina, *Proceedings,* 1869, pp. 37-48.

tees with power to elect their own successors, and the legislature was to elect six other trustees. The provision that a majority of the trustees were to be independent of the legislature was designed to insure the execution of the will according to the specifications of Clemson and to keep the institution out of politics, especially if the Negro should gain control of the state.[28] Tillman was delighted with this opportunity for carrying his idea to success. He immediately abandoned his intention of remaining in retirement and prepared to launch a campaign to induce the state to accept the bequest.

The will had been effective only two weeks, when Tillman, after a conference with members of the executive committee of the Farmers' Association, published an address demanding the establishment by the state of the agricultural college, "in that fortune had unexpectedly smiled upon us in the form of the munificent bequest of Mr. Clemson." "With consummate cunning and unblushing inconsistency," he added, "the friends of the University had taken advantage of the agitation for a separate agricultural college to build up the wonderful ten-student annex." While he expressed no intention of attacking the university as a place for liberal culture, he demanded that the subsidy for agricultural education which it re-

[28] Tillman MS. "The Origin of Clemson." The text of the Clemson will as taken from the records of Oconee county is published in *Clemson College Bulletin,* XII. No. 1 (March, 1916), pp. 23-25.

ceived from the national government be given to the new institution, the creation of which he asked. Hoping to carry into effect his plans through victory in the approaching election of 1888, he advised the people to "arouse themselves from their lethargy and to take a more active interest in political affairs." In order to avoid the return of a legislature like that of the previous year, he enjoined the people to beware of "demagogues and fence-straddlers and weak-kneed individuals without firmness of character or convictions of their own."[29]

Knowing how firmly his opponents were intrenched in the control of the Democratic party, Tillman soon became convinced that a change in the manner of nominating public officers was necessary in order to bring into play the full weight of the popular sentiment behind him. He prepared to ask the party to institute public debates between candidates for office and to substitute a direct system of primary elections for the prevailing system of choice through a convention. Accordingly, he induced the Democratic executive committee of Edgefield County, of which he was chairman, to record itself as favoring the first of these proposals. The Edgefield County convention—which was called to elect delegates to a state convention which, in turn, was called to

[29] For the address, Tillman Scrapbook, No. 1.

elect delegates to the national convention of that year—adopted his idea of a direct primary and sent him to Columbia with instructions to advocate it before the state convention.[30]

The most notable event of the state assemblage was Tillman's speech in favor of the primary. Although he knew that there was a great majority against his proposal, he did not hold himself in reserve, but boldly spoke in the midst of the enemy as sharply as he had written in his letters. "We are standing on the brink of a volcano that may at any time sweep everything before it," he cried. "I stand here as the representative of the people of South Carolina who stand for reform." The people for twenty years, he continued, had been tied hand and foot to the inaction of white unity because of the menace of the Negro. "But two years from now when there is full head on," he predicted, "you [the delegates] will be swept before the flood." "The majority of you do not represent the people of South Carolina. You represent rings and cliques from your different counties." When interrupted by cries of "Question!" from the indignant delegates, he cried, "You may gag me here, but I will meet you before the people." "When I think of the crimes," he concluded, "which have been committed in this hall [*i.e.*, the hall of the House of Representa-

[30] *News and Courier,* May 1, 1888.

tives], I shudder to enumerate them—financial extravagance, tricky practices. . . . The members have been bamboozled or affected in some way by Columbia water or whiskey, or by Charleston brains."

The speech failed of its immediate purpose, for the primary proposal was voted down by the large majority of 123. Yet the proposal that the candidates be given opportunity to address the people was provided for by the designation of places and dates for one such meeting in each congressional district. Moreover, Tillman's speech had a far-reaching effect upon the people. It helped to undermine their confidence in the convention system of nomination and demonstrated that their leader was as capable in the face of the enemy as he had been when protected by the isolation of his farm.[31]

In inaugurating the practice of joint debates between the candidates for public office, this convention added a distinctive institution to the political life of South Carolina. These meetings, or "one ring circuses" as they have been derisively called, filled a real need in the life of rural South Carolinians. They gave some relief from the monotony of country life in this time after the decline of the camp meeting and before the rise of

[31] For the proceedings of this convention, *News and Courier,* May 17, 1888; Columbia *Daily Register* and Fairfield *Herald and News,* May 18, 1888.

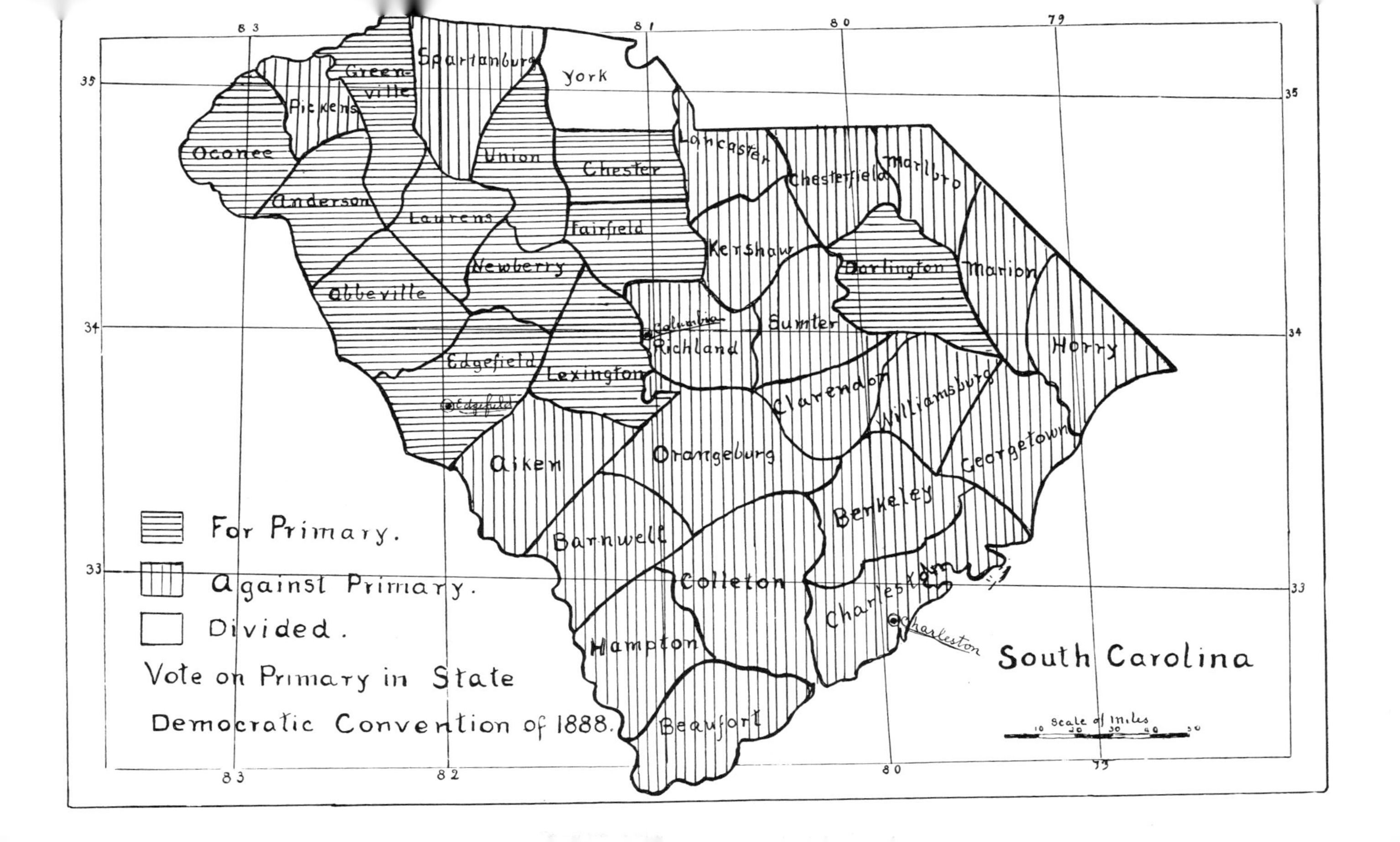

South Carolina
For Primary.
Against Primary.
Divided.
Vote on Primary in State
Democratic Convention of 1888.
Oconee
Pickens
Greenville
Spartanburg
York
Anderson
Laurens
Union
Chester
Lancaster
Chesterfield
Marlboro
Fairfield
Kershaw
Darlington
Marion
Newberry
Abbeville
Edgefield
Lexington
Richland
Columbia
Sumter
Horry
Clarendon
Williamsburg
Georgetown
Aiken
Orangeburg
Berkeley
Barnwell
Colleton
Charleston
Hampton
Beaufort
Scale of miles
10 20 30 40 50
35
34
33
83
82
81
80
79

the automobile. Around an improvised rostrum, partly shaded from the summer sun by a grove of oaks, most of the white men of the neighborhood, and such women as dared risk the possibility of coarse language from an immodest speaker or a brawl from whiskey-laden rowdies, would gather to hear jests and denunciations and even to receive advice and information concerning affairs of state from their favorite candidate. If there was promise of the opposing candidates engaging in a hot debate, the crowd often ran into the thousands. While these meetings may be justly criticized on the ground that they aroused passions and gave opportunity to smooth-tongued demagogues, it cannot be denied that these occasions gave the people a chance to meet face to face those from whom they were to select their governors, that this rough and tumble method of candidacy was an effective means of exposing the weaknesses and failings of the candidates, and that it was by means of these meetings that Tillman and others stirred the white masses of the state into making themselves important in politics.

Tillman, although not a candidate for any office, appeared at the first of these joint debates, which was held at the railroad station of Hodges in Abbeville County, July 20, 1888. His opponents were Governor Richardson and Lieutenant Governor Mauldin, who were, up to that time, the only candidates for the offices they held. Seven hundred enthusiastic admirers of Tillman sat on log-hewn seats to await their idol and the feast of barbecued kid and mutton which was to follow the speaking. In reply to the address of Richardson, Tillman spoke in a manner which delighted his hearers. He opened with an ironic regret for being forced to follow "the silver-tongued Governor, whose glowing words in praising South Carolina have stirred my heart." He followed with a series of denunciations and pleasantries. An example of the former was his designation of Dawson, who had written an editorial criticizing Tillman's speech before the Democratic convention, as "a buzzard who had escaped from the market house of Charleston and gone into the *News and Courier* office where it is spewing its slime on me." An example of his pleasantries was his story of a visit to the Columbia Club. He had been seized by the arm and taken to "this monstrous nice place", where he had been offered a strong drink, but had only taken a lemonade. "No wonder," he remarked amid laughter, "the corn bread and bacon fellows like it!" But the inclusion of such material as the foregoing did not prevent him from making statements concerning the constructive reforms he would accomplish. He made clear his desire to reform the legislature in order that the agricultural college might be built without de-

F. W. DAWSON

stroying the university as a school of liberal culture. The audience expressed its approval of his address by a vote of thanks.[32]

At the four other meetings of the canvass Tillman was the main issue. Although he did not attend the Greenville meeting, because he was not invited, each of the speakers took occasion to comment upon "the foul slanders" of which he was said to be guilty. Dawson, the editor of the *News and Courier,* appeared for the purpose of answering Tillman's Hodges speech.[33] Before a very sympathetic audience at Chester, Tillman answered those who claimed that he was in a conspiracy against the integrity of the Democratic party. "I hurl," he said to the excited gathering, "the imputation in their teeth and declare it a lie." When he engaged in a passage of words with Governor Richardson, the crowd jeered the latter. This was interpreted by the newspapers as an insult.[34] At Sumter Tillman was opposed by three speakers and a hostile crowd. Instead of modifying his onslaught in the face of jeers from the crowd and upbraidings from the speakers, he even became bolder than usual. He said to the audience: "Some have come here to see what sort of animal I am. I have neither hoofs nor horns, but I am a plain, simple farmer like yourself." In criti-

[32] N. G. Gonzales in *News and Courier,* July 21, 1888.
[33] *Greenville News,* July 25, 1888.
[34] *News and Courier.* July 23, 1888.

cizing Sumter County for electing delegates to the Democratic convention before he had spoken there, he said in anger, "I wish I had those delegates here to tell them my mind."[35]

The culmination of the canvass was his two speeches in Charleston, where he had gone to meet Dawson in debate. His first appearance was disappointing, due to the fact that Dawson was unavoidably absent attending to his duties as member of the executive committee of the national Democratic party. Nevertheless, Tillman, under the very shadow of St. Michael's, the church of the city's conservative aristocracy, in a stone's throw of the *News and Courier* office, and with four speakers as his opponents, achieved a personal triumph. He won a hearing from a hostile audience by the use of humor, was highly amused because the crowd fled when it mistook a drum beat for an earthquake,[36] and got much satisfaction because he was able to say that he "had come to Charleston not to make friends but to brush the cobwebs from over the people's eyes."[37]

More notable than this speech, however, was his return speech made on invitation of the element in the city hostile to the dominating influence

[35] *News and Courier,* August 2, 1888.

[36] The destructive earthquake of 1886 was fresh in the crowd's mind.

[37] *News and Courier,* August 5, 1888.

of Dawson and the local political machine. Again appearing on the same platform on which he had previously appeared, before an audience mostly hostile, he spoke of the city just as he felt. This means that his speech stands as an extraordinary example of rude boldness, for he, as an up-country farmer, could not be credited with any love for the low-country city of privilege and aristocratic conservatism. He began in this manner:

> You Charleston people are a peculiar people. If one-tenth of the reports which come to me are true, you are the most arrant set of cowards that ever drew the fresh air of heaven. You submit to a tyranny that is degrading to you as white men. . . . If anybody were to attempt this tyranny in Edgefield, I swear before Almighty God we would lynch him. The people of Charleston send legislators to Columbia not to legislate for you; they go there to make money.

Then followed an attack on Dawson:

> You [the people of Charleston] are cringing down in the mire because you are afraid of that newspaper down the street. Its editor bestrides the State like a colossus, while we poor men, whose boots he ain't fit to lick, are crawling under him seeking dishonored graves. He is the old man of the seas clinging around the neck of South Carolina, oppressing the people and stifling reform.

He had hardly finished these words when Dawson, amidst much confusion, dramatically mounted the platform and with much spirit answered "the defamer from Edgefield."[38]

[38] *News and Courier,* August 29, 1888.

This performance of Tillman had a lasting effect upon his career. Although he had spared no words in his characterization of the political situation in Charleston, he had spoken without effective interruption and had proved his mettle in the face of enemies. Charleston waited until after he retired to strike. Then several hundred patriotic citizens marched to the *News and Courier's* office to hear its editor denounce the "invader"; and the reply of the Charleston county was the election of a solid anti-Tillman delegation to the approaching state convention. A *News and Courier* editorial denounced Tillman as "the leader of the Adullamites, a people who carry pistols in their hip pockets, who expectorate upon the floor, who have no tooth brushes and comb their hair with their fingers."[39] Whatever the remainder of South Carolina might do, the Charlestonians resolved to wait many a year before looking with favor upon one who had so rudely insulted their city.

The canvass of the state gave Tillman great personal satisfaction, although he did not win a majority of the delegates to the nominating convention. He inspired enthusiasm everywhere, even provoking salvos of applause at Charleston. The hostility of the majority of that city found double compensation in the increased enthusiasm

[39] *News and Courier,* August 30, 1888.

which such hostility provoked among those of the up-country who were still conscious of the traditional hostility between the sections. Had the May convention initiated the primary system of elections instead of retaining the convention system, or even postponed the election of delegates to the nominating convention until after the canvass, it is likely that the man designated by Tillman would have become the governor of South Carolina. As the situation was, Tillman had to content himself with increased personal popularity, as many of the counties chose their delegates before the canvassers had reached their section of the state,[40] and Tillman's political managers had not as yet gained sufficient political experience to capture from veteran conservative leaders the management of a majority of the county conventions. In fact, early in July, Tillman had given up hope of controlling the convention.[41] But this did not prevent him from securing almost a majority of the delegates and an actual majority of the nominees of the party for the House of Representatives.

A necessary question at this point is, why was Tillman able to exert such a powerful hold on

[40] Fifteen counties had chosen their delegates before Tillman's second speech. Compiled from reports in *News and Courier*.

[41] In interviews. *News and Courier,* July 3, 1888. His opinion concerning the degree of his control over the people was expressed in the following declaration: "Give me a primary and I will run for Governor."

the white masses? One explanation is that the farmers for the first time in the history of the state were given the opportunity of being led by one who looked at life from their angle, was like them in personal appearance, and who expressed their ideas. In addition, the humorous and coarse manner in which he expressed himself was both interesting and appealing to a majority, who, close to the soil, were not too delicate in matters of taste. Although in manner he was as abusive and as unconventional as a Jacobin, his ideas, stripped of personalities and banter, were sufficiently constructive to give the farmers hope, and not sufficiently radical to frighten conservative landowners.

With almost half of the delegates on its side, the members of the Tillman faction pursued tactics in the Democratic nominating convention of 1888 similar to those pursued in 1886. They resolved to center upon a candidate for governor who was less objectionable to them than Governor Richardson. Their choice was Attorney General Joseph H. Earle. This was in the face of the fact that Earle's only part in the canvass of the past summer had been in the nature of vigorous speeches against Tillman, and in spite of the fact that he had expressed no desire to become a candidate in opposition to his administrative chief, whose successor two years thence conservative sentiment of the state would have him be. Although for a time

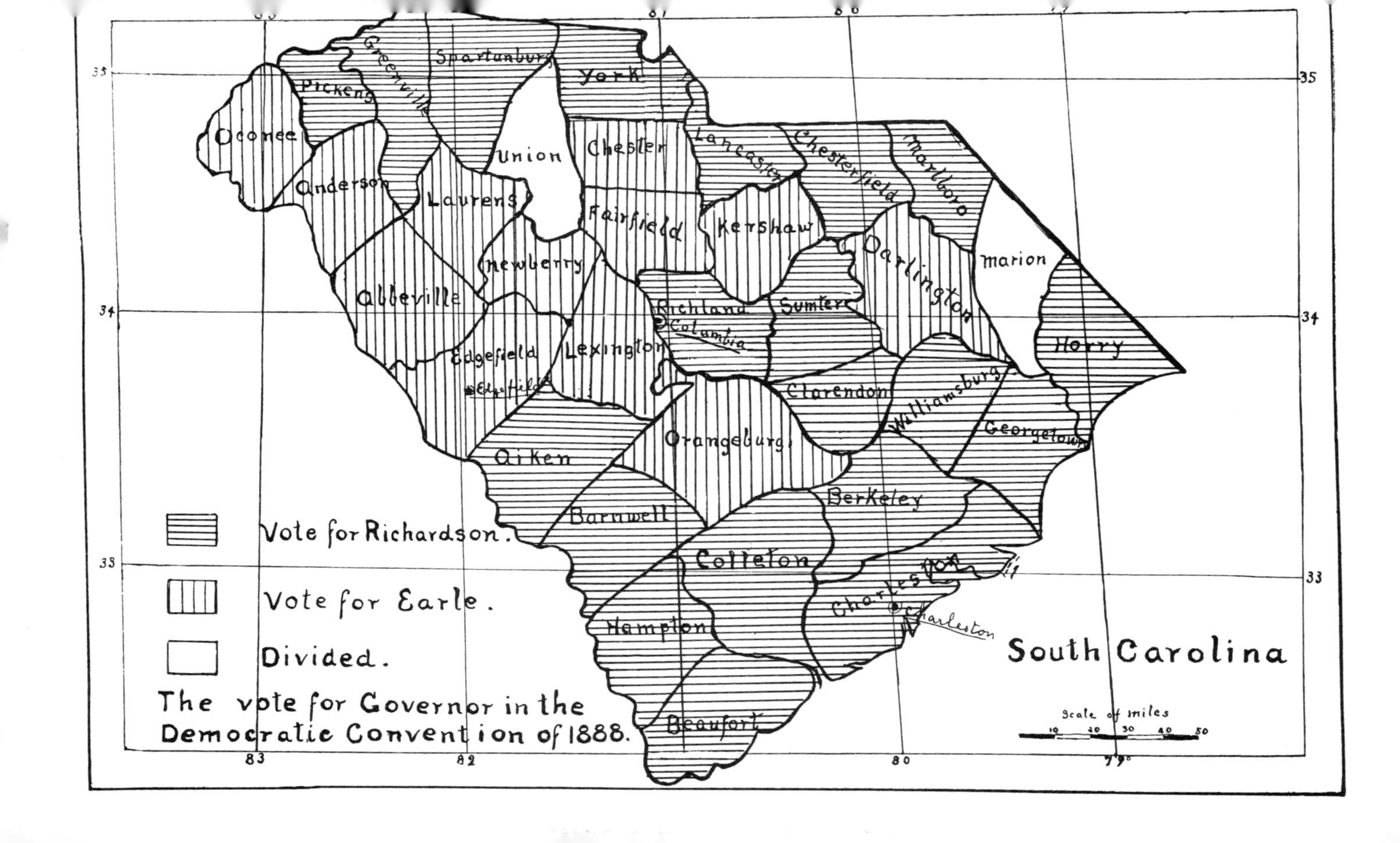
South Carolina
Vote for Richardson.
Vote for Earle.
Divided.
The vote for Governor in the Democratic Convention of 1888.
Scale of miles
10 20 30 40 50
Oconee
Pickens
Greenville
Spartanburg
York
Union
Chester
Lancaster
Chesterfield
Marlboro
Anderson
Laurens
Fairfield
Kershaw
Darlington
Marion
Newberry
Abbeville
Richland
Columbia
Sumter
Horry
Edgefield
Lexington
Clarendon
Williamsburg
Georgetown
Orangeburg
Aiken
Berkeley
Barnwell
Colleton
Charleston
Hampton
Beaufort
35
34
33
83
82
81
80
79°

he vacillated between accepting the tempting offer made him by Tillman and retaining the confidence of the conservatives,[42] on the eve of the convention he authorized the withdrawal of his name in case it was presented. Nevertheless, D. K. Norris, the Tillman floor leader, placed him in nomination. This was followed by an explicit statement from Earle's brother that the nomination under no circumstances would be accepted. However, Earle, in face of these adverse happenings, received 116 votes to Richardson's 195. Had he been willing to serve, his nomination by the party would have been more likely than that of Sheppard two years earlier. Tillman, although piqued at what he regarded as his "betrayal" by Earle, gracefully acknowledged his defeat and moved that the nomination of Richardson be made unanimous.[43]

He was defeated by an overwhelming vote in a second attempt to have the Democratic party adopt the primary system of nominating state officials. But he was victorious in securing the passage of a resolution requiring the Democratic chairman for each county to invite the candidates for state offices to hold joint meetings in their

[42] "The antagonism to Earle was at a boiling point," said Gonzales. *News and Courier,* September 7, 1888. Earle explained his conduct in the Sumter *Watchman and Southron,* November 21, 1888.

[43] For account of convention, see the *News and Courier,* September 6-8, 1888.

respective counties. Thus the system of joint debates, which had been inaugurated in each congressional district, became a county-to-county affair.

With a majority of ten on their side in the House of Representatives and with only two votes under a majority in the Senate, the Tillman leaders made the question as to whether the Clemson will should be accepted the center of discussion in the legislature of 1888. The opponents of the proposition believed that it was unwise for the state to become a partner in an undertaking over the majority of whose trustees it had no control, that the state should not accept the will in view of the fact that the heirs of Clemson were questioning its validity in court, and because Clemson was said to have been guilty of "licentious living." Yet, in spite of these arguments and of the opposition of excited galleries favorable to the university, the bill to accept the bequest passed the House by a substantial majority and the Senate through the vote of Lieutenant Governor Mauldin, who was called upon to break a tie.[44] But the bill did not immediately become law, because Governor Richardson, in view of the fact that the legislature adjourned within three days after the bill was sent to him, exercised

[44] For the debate, see the *News and Courier*, December 16-20, 1888; for the vote, *House Journal*, 1888, p. 251; *Senate Journal*, 1888, p. 263. The bill passed the House by vote of 67 to 48.

his constitutional right to hold it in suspense until another session. Meanwhile, circumstances fortunate for the bill developed. The delay of the Governor made him the target of much popular criticism; a student publication of the university admitted that at that institution "the temptation of more liberal courses are a continual drawback to the pursuit of agricultural studies;"[45] in April the United States circuit court declared the will valid.[46] The Governor, impressed by these facts, signed the bill in November.[47]

The principal task of the session of 1889 was the framing of a law that would give the proposed Clemson College the fullest opportunity for development with the least injury to the state university. W. C. Benet, a Scotch lawyer and schoolmaster from Abbeville, skillfully accomplished this task, although the university was divested of the Federal assistance to its agricultural annex. The Clemson bill passed the House without a division.[48] In the Senate it was declared to be "the big humbug" of Tillman, "the defeated crusader," and Clemson was declared to have been "a vanity-stricken, miserable agnos-

[45] St. Julian Grimké, *University Carolinian,* January, 1889, pp. 96-97.

[46] *Lee* vs. *Simpson, 37 Federal Reporter,* 12.

[47] Act of November 20, 1889; *Acts and Joint Resolutions,* 1889, pp. 277-279.

[48] *House Journal,* 1889, p. 31.

tic."[49] But it easily passed and immediately received the signature of the Governor.[50]

The new agricultural sentiment in the legislature of 1888-89 found expression in various successful and unsuccessful attempts to force into law other measures designed to benefit the farmers. On the initiative of Edward McCrady, the historian of South Carolina, a law was passed regulating and protecting primary elections.[51] This act prepared the way for the acceptance by the Democratic party of the primary system of nominations, which that party had rejected in the previous summer. Over the protest of railroad interests, the farmers were able to effect the enactment of a law giving the railroad commission authority to fix freight and passenger rates.[52] However, the bill designed to prohibit members of the legislature from receiving free railroad passes, in order to lessen the influence of railroads in politics, failed.[53] It was hinted that too many members were already in receipt of that benefit. Efforts to reduce the salary of public officials were unsuccessful; a bill to reduce the salaries of judges, which was sponsored by farmers who

[49] From the debate of December 19, 1889, *News and Courier*, December 20, 1889.

[50] *Senate Journal*, 1889, p. 485; *Acts and Joint Resolutions*, 1889, pp. 299-302.

[51] *Ibid.*, 1889, pp. 10-12.

[52] *Ibid.*, 1889, pp. 64-66.

[53] *House Journal*, 1889, p. 63 of index.

cherished strong prejudices against a profession to which lawyers only were eligible, passed the House, but not the Senate.[54] A resolution of protest against the salaries paid to the professors in the university was championed by those who felt that that institution had more teachers than the number of its students justified.[55] But this move likewise failed. These efforts were in keeping with Tillman's complaint against the burden of taxation and the alleged extravagance in the public administration. The attempt to take the collection of the state tax on fertilizers out of the hands of the agricultural commission and the attempt to elect Tillman and the other nominees of the farmers to that commission failed.[56] Although the constitution of 1868 was declared "unfit for a white man to live under" and its retention an evidence of "pandering to Yankee sentiment," the resolution for the calling of a constitutional convention did not receive the necessary two-thirds vote of the Senate.[57]

Before considering in the next chapter the activities of Tillman, which led to his final success, we may well summarize at this point the results of the agitation which he had begun at Bennettsville, in 1885. He had proved himself to be a writer

[54] *Senate Journal,* 1889, p. 286.

[55] In 1888 the number of students was 170; the number of professors, 25.

[56] *House Journal,* 1889, pp. 218-222.

[57] *Senate Journal,* 1889, p. 142.

and speaker with ability to arouse among the white agricultural masses of the state an absorbing devotion to his personality and to his program. This made possible the certain realization in the near future of his cherished idea, the agricultural college. But, at the same time, we should not forget that he had suffered many disappointments. His manners and his sayings had aroused the bitterest personal resentment on the part of the element which was still intrenched in political power. His attempts to elect a governor even partly in favor of his program had twice ended in failure. His program of reform, with the single exception of the agricultural college, had been voted down at four successive sessions of the general assembly. The realization that his displeasing personality had been more responsible for these defeats than any other single reason had been the cause of much bitter personal reflection, out of which at one time had grown the resolution to place the management of the farmers' interests in the hands of others. Yet no defeat could divest him of the belief in the essential justice of his cause and in the ability of the class which he represented to capture the state government, or of the persistent energy with which he pursued that which he had set out to accomplish.

CHAPTER V

THE ELECTION OF 1890

As there was little chance of influencing further the hold-over legislature of 1889, the executive committee of the Farmers' Association resolved not to hold a meeting in the fall of that year. Instead, a convention of the farmers and their supporters was called to meet after the adjournment of the legislature for the purpose of effecting plans through which the conventions and elections scheduled for the summer and fall of 1890 might be captured. Tillman, with the aid of G. W. Shell[1] and John L. M. Irby,[2] two sagacious and popular leaders of Laurens County, prepared an address and program for this convention. He was induced to abandon his pledge not to become a candidate for public office, in order that he might be presented to the convention as a suitable candi-

[1] Shell's popularity was based on the fact that he was genial and capable, that he had served as a Confederate soldier, had been suspected of being involved in the killing of Crews, a political renegade, and had long served as clerk of court of Laurens County.

[2] Irby's prestige rested on the fact that he came from a good family and was possessed of an attractive and over-mastering personality.

date for the Democratic gubernatorial nomination.[3]

Early in the new year the memorable "Shell Manifesto"—written by Tillman but taking its name from the President of the Farmers' Association—bade the farmers meet in convention, March 27. Delegates were to be elected in very much the same manner as those to the Democratic conventions. In order to anticipate the charge that such a political convention, called to meet in a political year before the time of the regular Democratic convention, had as its purpose the disruption of that party and the consequent abandonment of the dearly cherished principle of white unity, the farmers were very careful to give assurance that they had no desire to bolt the Democratic party and would subordinate their program to that party even if its convention decided against them. They felt that a March convention was necessary in order to remedy certain evils which were a part of the political organization of South Carolina. It was claimed that, since the time of the Lords Proprietors of Carolina, South Carolina had been controlled by an "aristocratic oligarchy." This oligarchy, it was claimed, found expression in a "Ring" composed of the chief beneficiaries of "the existing institutions"—the university, the

[3] For the inception of the convention idea, see Shell's address before it and a letter of Robert Smith published in the *News and Courier,* September 2, 1890.

G. W. SHELL

military academy at Charleston, the agricultural bureau, and the Columbia Club. The ambition of this group, the charge continued, "was to keep all that they could get with the hope that the people would again fall into their accustomed apathy," to stifle progress, to increase expenditures for the benefit of its members, and to keep political pensioners in office even after they had passed the age of usefulness. When a friend of the people arose, this oligarchy bought him with office. The farmers were told that it was necessary to resort to more intensive methods of political organization in order to wrench from "the aristocratic coterie" the control of the state Senate and executive offices, so that in the future it would be impossible for the legislature to be "bamboozled and debauched" and the railroad commission "tamed." "Fellow Democrats," was the ringing conclusion of the manifesto,

> do not these things cry out for a change? Is it not opportune, when there is no national election, for the common people, who redeemed South Carolina from radical rule, to take charge of it? Can we afford to leave it longer in the hands of those who, wedded to ante-bellum ideas, but with little of the ante-bellum patriotism and honor, are running it for the benefit of a few families and for the benefit of a ring of selfish politicians?[4]

Many South Carolinians received this call with misgivings. Although it was no more radical in

[4] Text of the Shell Manifesto, Tillman Scrapbook, No. 2.

its content than previous Tillman pronouncements, conservatives were outraged because of the caustic manner in which it was phrased. A large number of the people, perhaps a majority, were positively alarmed over the possibility that the convention would enter the election without the coöperation of that section of the Democratic party not in sympathy with the Shell Manifesto. The fact that the manifesto carried a positive statement that the decision of the Democratic convention would be obeyed was not sufficient to quiet a population which held in utmost horror the possibility of a return to Negro rule through a break in the ranks of the white party. Hoyt, the Democratic state chairman, issued a solemn warning concerning the evils of an independent movement, and perhaps even a majority of the delegates elected to the convention by county farmers' associations were either instructed to vote against the nomination of candidates or were personally convinced of the lack of wisdom of nominations.[5]

Notwithstanding these misgivings, at the appointed hour of noon, March 27, Chairman Shell called to order the so-called March convention. There were present the large number of 233 delegates. It was, in the opinion of Gonzales, "one of the queerest deliberative bodies that has even as-

[5] By March 5, of those counties which had elected delegates, six had instructed against nominations and six in favor; nine were undecided. Summary in *News and Courier,* March 5, 1890.

sembled in the State House." All professions were represented, but a great majority were farmers. The matter of principal concern was, of course, whether there should be immediate nominations for governor and other state offices. The forces for immediate nominations were organized under the leadership of Shell, Irby, and Senator Talbert; while the forces opposed to nominations were led by J. J. Dargan, who had already, in several farmers' conventions, manifested a vigorous opposition to Tillman. Irby won the first victory for immediate nominations by effecting the election of Talbert as permanent chairman and by causing the convention to instruct the committee on credentials not to admit delegates likely to be obstructive. The committee, however, did seat some contested delegations opposed to nomination. This was followed by a motion from a delegate from Edgefield,[6] "that for the purpose of educating and arousing the people we will proceed to suggest candidates for Governor and Lieutenant Governor who favor the Convention's platform, and ask that those who disagree with us do likewise. . . . Let us have a full and fair discussion within the party lines." This motion caused two hours of confusion and fierce debate, followed by cries for Tillman. In

[6] A. E. Padgett.

determined words Tillman signified his willingness to be the convention's candidate for governor:

> I do not want to be the nominee, but if you ask me to fight for it, I will fight as long as I have a dollar left and the health with which to fight. I will put myself against the combined intellect of the Ring. . . . But, I say to you that the reform element in South Carolina has reached the Rubicon. . . . If you ask me to lead the fight, you call on me to lead a forlorn hope, but you will have at your head the only man who has the brains, the nerve and the ability to organize the common people against the aristocracy.[7]

After this address a period of wild confusion ensued. Chairman Talbert had great difficulty in quieting both himself[8] and the assembly. He then ordered a vote. The first tally indicated the defeat of the forces for immediate nomination by one vote. Irby, now working with Talbert, undertook the task of changing apparent defeat into victory. He effected a draw by throwing out a contested vote, and the declaration of an actual majority by using the weight of his positive personality to force several delegates to change their votes.[9] Had the opposition leaders been as dexterous as Irby and Talbert, they could have

[7] On account of the element of self-praise which entered into these remarks much controversy arose as to their exact nature. I use here Tillman's own revision as published in a letter to the *News and Courier,* November 5, 1890.

[8] Talbert incurred much criticism because he made a speech himself.

[9] The vote as finally declared was 120 in favor to 114 in opposition.

won, for the opposition appears to have had the greater latent strength. Irby followed the declaration of victory by proposing, in a voice that rang high and clear, the name of Tillman for governor. "Shame on the party," he said, "that stabbed Mart Gary in the back. We owe Edgefield something." The nomination was carried by acclamation without articulate opposition. Tillman accepted, and the convention adjourned in short order.[10]

It can not be denied that the manner in which Irby managed the convention was high-handed and perhaps served to defeat the free will of the majority of the delegates. Yet he had only done what the average presiding officer of a Democratic or Republican convention was in the habit of doing: he suppressed members of the body who claimed a right to express themselves in a convention called for a purpose with which they were not in sympathy. This element had the right, which it no doubt exercised, of expressing itself against Irby and Tillman within the bounds of the Democratic party, just as elements expelled from Democratic and Republican conventions express themselves in general elections.

Why did Tillman abandon his original promise of never becoming a candidate for public office and

[10] For the proceedings, see the Columbia *Daily Register* and Gonzales in the *News and Courier,* March 27-29, 1890.

plunge so deeply into political life that he held public office for the remainder of his days? There are several explanations of this change of front. Substitute candidates had twice failed him. Both he and his backers felt that he was the only person in South Carolina capable of achieving victory for his "forlorn hope." It is true that he personally was largely responsible for the vigorous opposition which his cause would encounter. But he possessed other personal qualities capable of counteracting the aversion for his personality. At the age of forty-three he was in the prime of physical and mental vigor, had to his credit the successes of the campaign of 1888, and had in the five years of his agitations created an enthusiasm for himself among the white masses greater than that enjoyed by any South Carolinian before or since. He understood the class and sectional divisions in the state and knew how to exploit them for political purposes. In addition, there can be little doubt that Ben Tillman desired the emoluments and honors of public office as eagerly as did some of the "broken-down aristocrats" whom he criticised. It was but natural for a hungry farmer, who never claimed idealism and unselfishness as among his virtues, to want advancement.

In addition to the personal qualities which Tillman had in his favor, he had other influences on his side. The Farmers' Association—known after the March convention as the Reform Movement—was a well organized political machine with ramifications extending into every county of the state. Irby, as his political manager, was as sagacious as the most experienced conservative politicians. As candidates for the other executive offices, the ablest among his followers were designated.[11] Farmers turned politicians, and lawyers who saw in the new movement opportunity to better themselves were ready to give Irby active and capable assistance. A daily newspaper, the *Charleston World,* which had been founded by the political faction of that city that had invited Tillman to speak in 1888, was induced to become the Tillman organ. In addition, the Farmers' Alliance, an association of national importance, lent its powerful support.

The nature of the support which the Alliance gave Tillman demands attention at this point. This movement had been introduced into South Carolina in 1887[12] and by 1889 had a state or-

[11] Eugene B. Gary, the nephew of Martin Gary, became candidate for lieutenant-governor; James E. Tindal, a wealthy planter educated in Germany, became candidate for secretary of state; Y. J. Pope, a Confederate veteran, became candidate for attorney general; W. D. Mayfield, a successful educational administrator, candidate for superintendent of education; W. C. T. Bates, an experienced banker, candidate for state treasurer; and Hugh Farley, who had been a devoted friend of Martin Gary, candidate for adjutant and inspector general.

[12] The Great Sea Alliance was its first local organization in the state.

ganization with 740 local divisions. Although its ostensible purpose was the promotion of more attractive farm life and of coöperative buying among farmers, the Alliance in South Carolina, as in other states, could not withstand the temptation to enter politics. It was easy for the popular Alliance organizer to become a popular politician, and the popularity of politicians and political agitations were much more effective in attracting the general public to the organization than were agitations concerned only with rural betterment and coöperative buying. The average Alliance farmer of that day, believing that the intervention of the state in his behalf was a very effective and quick means through which his complaints might be remedied, naturally sought the control of the state government. But this sacrifice to politics of the original purposes of the organization transformed it into a noisy political machine, sure to go out of existence as soon as its leaders got political office and the rank and file were no longer interested in the passing political agitations which its leaders emphasized. Tillman, fearing the strength of the Alliance in politics and believing that it could better accomplish its purpose as a non-political organization, urged it to steer clear of politics.[13] When he saw that his advice was not to be taken, he, as a sensible politi-

[13] The Edgefield *Chronicle,* May 4, 1891.

cal opportunist, joined forces with the Alliance. He became first president of the Edgefield branch, and such prominent Tillman leaders as D. K. Norris, Jasper Talbert, and E. T. Stackhouse became prominent leaders in the Alliance. While this organization was a potent influence in securing the success of Tillman, to say, as does its historian,[14] that Tillman's election in 1890 was due to the Alliance is to ignore the unique social conditions which caused discontent in South Carolina, the force of Tillman's personality, and the agitations which he began three years before that organization entered the state.[15]

Meanwhile, the element within the Democratic party opposed to Tillman prepared to meet him in the county-to-county canvass scheduled for the coming summer. Those among the farmers dissatisfied with the decision of the March convention declared in conference: "We as agriculturists will not permit our occupation to be degraded by a spoilsman's machine." No formal nomination was made, as such a procedure had been declared an evidence of disloyalty to the Democratic party.[16] Nevertheless, the conservative classes united on Joseph H. Earle as their candidate for governor. His selection was considered as

[14] H. R. Chamberlain, *The Farmers' Alliance,* p. 28.

[15] The history of the Alliance in South Carolina is given in W. Scott Morgan, *History of the Wheel and Alliance,* pp. 326-7; S. J. Buck, *The Agrarian Crusade,* pp. 111-123.

[16] The Charleston *World,* April 24; May 21, 1890.

the necessary reward for having sacrificed his chances for nomination in 1888 in the interest of Governor Richardson. The independent conservative candidate was General James Bratton.

The choice of Earle was excellent. The fact that he had been a poor boy who had risen to prominence through hard work, that he had been a zealous advocate of the Democratic cause in the litigation growing out of Reconstruction, and that as attorney general under Richardson he had defended that administration against the attacks of Tillman, gave him great prestige. Possessed of curly locks, deeply set eyes, and an imposing figure, he was personally most attractive. Being a man of measured terms and even temper, he was not likely to lose his self-control in the face of Tillman's clever onslaughts. Undoubtedly he was the most formidable antagonist Tillman ever had in the many debates in which he engaged on the South Carolina hustings. But this does not mean that Earle was a match for his wiry antagonist. His very capabilities worked against him. His quiet dignity and constructive zeal for the welfare of the state were not satisfying retorts for the sarcasm, ridicule, and scoffs which Tillman offered the turbulent South Carolina democracy of 1890. Neither polished language nor a handsome figure was a fitting substitute among the rustic majority for the plain language of the farm which

JOSEPH H. EARLE

Tillman used and the rustic appearance with which he was endowed. "Tillman is one of us," reasoned the humble farmer; "Earle belongs to another class."[17]

The canvass was opened by a debate between Tillman and Earle held at Anderson, May 10, before an audience of about 1500, a large majority of whom were Tillman partisans.[18] Tillman opened his address with an explanation of his personal characteristics:

> I would have the people look me in the eye to see what sort of a man I am. . . . Judging from the newspaper reports, many of you cannot realize that such an insignificant man can be Tillman. . . . If I had no peculiarities, perhaps I would be an insignificant and unknown man. I am what I am, and God made me what I am, and therefore, if this conglomeration of flesh and bones becomes a factor in South Carolina, it will be by reason of my peculiarities. I am left handed, and I have written with the left paw. I am one-eyed. But some say that I can see more with that one eye than some men with a dozen.

He denied that he had manipulated the March convention in his favor or that he wished to destroy white political unity. He attacked the management of the state university, and the agricultural department, and he accused the

[17] For the facts of Earle's life see *Descriptive Review of South Carolina,* III. 223-224. For an interesting comparison of the two men, see L. H. Pattillo in the Augusta *Chronicle,* June 6, 15, 1890.

[18] This meeting was held under the auspices of the town of Anderson, before the regular canvass, under the auspices of the Democratic party, opened.

legislature of "perjury" for failure to reapportion legislative representation. He was unsparing in his criticism of "the greedy old city of Charleston," "the glorious city of Columbia," and Beaufort, "a niggerdom"—that is, those communities which were most hostile to him.

Earle, in reply, declared that the March convention had initiated a selfish class movement and that Tillman was a common office-seeker bent upon his own personal advantage. The speaker was greatly handicapped by the rude interruptions of Tillman and the excited outbursts of the crowd provoked by the words which passed between the two candidates. While he showed cool determination and ability to withstand these onslaughts, he showed no evidence of qualities likely to gain the sympathy of his audience.[19]

The canvass of other counties of the up-country was featured by demonstrations in favor of Tillman of such a turbulent nature that the opposition candidates were not given fair opportunities to state their cause. These demonstrations reached a climax at Laurens, the home of Shell and Irby. A huge crowd of men, women, and children, decorated with badges proclaiming the fact that they were for Tillman, began to arrive on the scene of

[19] *News and Courier*, Charleston *World*, and Augusta *Chronicle*, May 11, 1890.

I used three newspaper accounts for the events of this canvass: *News and Courier*, anti-Tillman; *World*, pro-Tillman; and Augusta *Chronicle*, inclined to neutrality.

the speaking before day. When the object of their admiration arrived, they cheered and danced with joy and bore him on their shoulders to the speakers' stand. "If mortal man," said an observer,[20] "can arouse his fellow beings to a higher pitch of enthusiasm than did Tillman, it would be a plain act of absolute worship." Amidst shouts of "Give us Tillman" and "Bring out the one-eyed plowboy," General Bratton vainly tried to be heard. Deafening howls greeted Earle's attempt to arraign Tillman. Although Tillman and Shell, the chairman of the meeting, attempted to quiet the crowd, the gathering adjourned without the farmer's opponents being given a hearing.[21]

Enraged at the discourtesies shown Earle and Bratton, the conservatives resolved, if possible, to humiliate Tillman when he arose to speak at Columbia, the stronghold of his enemies. Accordingly a crowd of 1500, ninety per cent. of whom were hostile to the farmer,[22] gathered in the city auditorium to rebuke him. Many openly bore arms, believing he was so cowardly that he could be frightened and disgraced by a show of force. Senators Hampton and Butler[23] and other leaders

[20] *Charleston Sun,* June 12, 1890.

[21] For this and the three preceeding meetings, see the *News and Courier,* the Charleston *World,* and the Augusta *Chronicle,* June 10-14, 1890.

[22] Estimate of the Augusta *Chronicle.*

[23] Both were invited by the executive committee of the Democratic party. Butler did not accept.

of conservative opinion were invited to lend prestige to the rebuke. With such a show of "free discussion," remarked John C. Haskell, a leading citizen of Columbia, "South Carolina will spew this vile thing [Tillman] out of her mouth, this creature who has slandered his mother State and accused falsely the white men who served her in 1876." Tillman's only partisans in the audience were the stalwart Irby at his side and a small contigent of "guano boys" from Edgefield.

Hampton abandoned a vacation tour of Canada in order to be present. The contrast between the two South Carolinians, Hampton and Tillman, who on this day were to contend for the good will of the people was most striking. Hampton was possessed of the polish of three generations of aristocratic culture; he was handsome and large, smartly dressed, and given to the polite phrases of the southern orator; he had served brilliantly in the war and had served well in 1876. The people had been taught to believe that he was a veritable grand old man of South Carolina. Tillman was rude, rough in appearance, possessed of a record of no service in the Confederate cause and only obscure service in 1876. Although it may not have been evident on this memorable day, he was the superior of Hampton in the game which the latter had elected to play with him. The great man was a kindly orator of ordinary ability, with scant

WADE HAMPTON

understanding of how he had been made governor in 1876 and of the social forces which Tillman represented. Tillman, as we have already said, understood conditions in his state and knew the manners and type of speech necessary to make him master of its destiny. Hampton was a representative of the glory of the past; Tillman, the hope of the future. The former, in abandoning the rôle of a neutral moderator of the affairs of white South Carolina in order that he might take sides, may have acted from a sense of duty; but his action was fruitless and resulted in his own undoing.

The address of General Hampton, as was characteristic of the man, was moderate, although it was a cold moderation which cut Tillman deeply. "When I saw that a South Carolina audience could insult General Bratton," he said, in reference to the Laurens meeting, "I thought, good God, have all the memories of '61 been forgotten?" "Shoulder to shoulder I implore you men of South Carolina, not to forget the past," he said, in reference to the belief that Tillman would destroy white unity. "It is useless to say that we are all Democrats when you do things that will divide us."

Tillman, in reply, was not abashed. Although pale, he spoke with the vigor of former occasions. Addressing the audience, he said, "You of the

[Democratic] convention have been merely damming the water back and this little Columbia dam is not going to stop the freshet." Amidst the hisses and howls of his hearers, he contrasted the virtue of the ante-bellum government with the sins of the government of 1890, "which is composed of men who seek positions for money." The most dramatic moment of the day, and perhaps the most trying moment of Tillman's career, was when A. C. Haskell, who had lost an eye in the Civil War and who was a brother of J. C. Haskell, arose to question Tillman concerning the most sensitive portion of his career—his record in the Civil War. Amidst much confusion Haskell asked:

"What age were you when the war ended; honest now; true age?"

"Seventeen," answered Tillman.

In order to convict his witness of having failed in his duty to the Confederacy, a crime which the average South Carolinian of that day did not easily forget, Haskell said, "The law called him at sixteen and patriotism put thousands in the army at fifteen." During this colloquy many brandished their weapons, either through sheer excitement or in the belief that such a ruse would frighten Tillman into cowardly conduct.

But Tillman, instead of wilting, rose to a defiant rage. Shaking a finger in the face of his interlocutor, he told of the loss of his eye and the consequent illness which prevented his service, and then said: "I can call upon as good a general as you, Haskell, to tell the part the Tillman family took in the War."

The general was Ellison Capers, the beloved rector of Trinity Church, Columbia, and later Episcopal Bishop of South Carolina, who sat among those designed to rebuke Tillman. Capers, in order to sustain the memory of one of his officers, came to the rescue of the hard-pressed speaker, to whom he was adverse, saying:

> When I am asked to bear testimony to the heroic gallantry of one of the brave men of my regiment, God forbid that I should keep silent. Jim Tillman [Ben's brother] was the oriflamme of my regiment.

This relieved the tension with Tillman triumphant, although the intervention of Hampton was necessary to bring sufficient order for Tillman to be heard. Then he closed his address with defiant flings at his opponents. To Hampton he said: "The grand mogul here, who ruled supremely and grandly, cannot terrify me. I do not come from such blood as that." "When any man comes here," he finally said to Haskell and the audience, "and talks about my record, I simply spew him out at the mouth. The Democratic party is full of leprosy. . . . About two-thirds of you want office if you can get it."

Then, protected by Irby, he left. Although the day had not been his, he had proved his mettle. No sensible man could thereafter make the ugly insinuation that he was a coward.[24]

The Tillmanites, angered by the manner in which their chief had been treated in Columbia, executed vengeance at Aiken. Senator Hampton was made the butt of their wrath. Although he spoke on invitation from the Democratic authorities of Aiken County, he began his address amidst indecorous cries of "Put him out," and when he intimated the fear that the Tillman movement would destroy white unity, the howls became so great that he was forced to sit down.[25]

Retaliation for the humilitations visited upon Hampton and Bratton was sought at Winnsboro, the home of Bratton. Tillman, in spite of the efforts of Bratton to bring quiet, was forced to take his seat without speaking. When his partisans saw his discomfiture, they rushed to the platform, lifted him on their shoulders, and swore that he must be allowed to speak. Then came a dead calm and a counter rush from the anti-Tillmanites. Because of the determination of the two groups, remarked an observer,[26] "at no meeting of the past series has such bad blood been

[24] For the Columbia meeting, see the *News and Courier,* the Charleston *World,* and the Augusta *Chronicle,* June 25, 1890.

[25] Augusta *Chronicle,* June 28, 1890.

[26] *Ibid.,* July 2, 1890.

displayed or a culmination of such desperate character threatened."

At Florence, Tillman resorted for the first time to one of the most effective means of proving that the audience was friendly to him—the so-called "hand primary." "Who of you are for Bratton," he cried, "hold up your hands." A few hands went up. When he applied the same question concerning Earle, a larger number went up. When he asked concerning himself, a veritable sea of hands was raised.[27]

Tillman insisted on calling the name of each state senator on his list of "perjured senators" who had refused to vote for the re-apportionment of representation in the legislature in spite of the fact that the senators had taken an oath to obey the constitution, which required the re-apportionment of representation every tenth year. Such a direct charge of perjury made against so influential a local personage as a state senator aroused the bitterest hostility against the accuser in every county in which the charge was made. For example, Senator Laurence Youmans of Barnwell, at Ridgeway, almost caused a fight when Tillman refused to retract this charge.[27a] At Hampton, a friend of the accused senator from that county, with loud oaths in his mouth, attempted to advance upon the speaker. He was

[27] Augusta *Chronicle,* July 4, 1890.

[27a] *News and Courier,* June 8, 1890.

only restrained from a possible act of violence by the interference of Tillman's friends, an act which almost broke up the meeting.[28]

The county-to-county canvass had been a great triumph for Tillman and his cause. Only at Columbia, Winnsboro, Sumter, Charleston, and a few other towns of the lowlands was a majority of those who attended the meetings against him. A majority, no doubt, was on his side before the canvass began; the matchless manner in which he met those who opposed him served to increase this majority and to make him the idol of the white democracy. He was loved for his wit, his aggressiveness in the face of the enemy, and his ability to ridicule the institutions and individuals he professed to despise. He said little about program and principles, for the noisy democracy was only interested in banter and personalities. He reserved, as we shall see, his sober program for future consideration.

Recognizing the nomination of Tillman as a not unlikely possibility,[29] the conservative leaders of the Democratic party met in council a month before the canvass was over to devise plans by which such an eventuality might be averted. An element of this assembly favored a declaration not

[28] Augusta *Chronicle,* July 12, 1890.

[29] As early as June 10, 108 delegates favorable to Tillman had been elected. Compilation from the *News and Courier,* June, 1890.

to support Tillman in case he won the nomination. But more conservative counsel prevailed. The assembly contented itself with the ambiguous announcement that it favored the election of officers "who would favor the State and not themselves," and with the demand for a primary. The answer of the Tillman leaders to this demand was the only natural reply that could have been made. "The campaign," said W. C. Benet,[30] "was begun on the basis of a nominating convention, and it is not to be expected that Tillman will consent to surrender that which he has already gained and fight the battle over again in the primaries."

When the time approached for the Democratic convention of August 10 for the purpose of making the rules of the party,[31] the anti-Tillman majority of the executive committee, seeing that if the usual routine of such a convention was followed the nomination of Tillman was inevitable, resolved upon an unusual line of procedure. It undertook to force a primary for the election of delegates to the scheduled nominating convention by declaring that the August convention was called "for the sole and exclusive purpose of determining whether or not delegates to the State Nominating Convention, scheduled for Septem-

[30] *Keowee Courier,* July 26, 1890.

[31] In an election year it was customary to hold two conventions—the first for the purpose of making the rules of the party, the second for nominations.

ber, be elected by primary, and for no other purpose." The purpose of the committee was to deny the first convention the right of allowing the same county conventions which had elected it to elect the delegates to the second convention. When the assembled convention, by a majority of two hundred, exercised its undoubted sovereign right of over-riding the instructions of its executive committee, the anti-Tillman delegates—those from Richland, Charleston, Beaufort, and Sumter—withdrew. Then, under the leadership of Irby, a new constitution was made, a new executive committee with Irby as chairman was created, and a convention, to be elected by the same county conventions which had elected the convention in session, was called.[32]

In the interval between the two conventions the anti-Tillmanites, instead of openly breaking with the party, declared the proceedings of the first convention illegal.[33] The Chairman of the old executive committee denied that his organization had been superseded and continued to issue manifestos in its name. The *News and Courier*[34] declared that the delegates then being elected for the nominating convention "will have no right to take part in the proceedings of the Convention."

[32] For the proceedings of this convention, see the *News and Courier*, Charleston *World*, Augusta *Chronicle*, and Columbia *Daily Register*, August 14-15, 1890.

[33] *News and Courier*, August 6, 1890.

[34] *Ibid.*, August 21, 1890.

The same men who in conference the previous month had petitioned for a primary were, in a second conference, unanimous in condemning the action of the August convention and in commending the delegates who had withdrawn from that assembly. Although, in their published address, no intimation was given that a majority of the conference would not support the actions of the nominating convention, a bold minority, behind closed doors, gave notice that there were white men in South Carolina who would bolt the traditional party of their race in case Tillman was nominated.[35]

The nomination convention met on its appointed date with the Tillman delegates in even a larger majority than they had been in the previous convention.[36] Tillman and the entire Tillman ticket were nominated without opposition. The minority contented itself with protests, ominous of the fact that the struggle for the control of the state government had still another phase. A. C. Haskell served notice that he regarded the proceedings of the convention as "illegal and void." The unseated Fairfield delegation, when extended seats on the floor of the convention, indignantly rejected the offer and marched out of the hall with a red jacket, symbolic of its claim to represent the

[35] Charleston *World,* August 27, 1890.

[36] There were 269 Tillman delegates to 40 anti-Tillmanites.

Hampton Democracy of 1876, borne high, while the gallery cheered.[37]

The logical sequel to Haskell's declaration was the organization of an independent movement, which pretended to be the proper representative of the Democratic party, whose functions Tillman was said to have usurped. Although Haskell acted against the advice of his brother and the more conservative faction of the anti-Tillmanites and against the traditions of white unity, he felt that he had sufficient reason to lead the fight. A man of good family, a graduate of South Carolina College, a veteran of the Civil War, a lawyer, a bank president, and a man of deep prejudices and of a spirited devotion to the interests of his class, he hated the man who had scoffed at the traditional, who had been a rude traducer of his friends, and who would pass laws to the detriment of lawyers and business men. "I will not vote for Mr. Tillman," he declared in the famous manifesto of the Haskellites,[38] "and I contend that no Democrat should vote for him." He then gave his reasons for his intention. The Shell Manifesto was hostile to the Democratic party. Tillman had charged the state government with "dishonesty, corruption and perjury"; the convention had violated the constitution of the party. "Technically, there-

[37] For the proceedings of this convention, see the *News and Courier,* and Charleston *World,* September 16, 1890.

[38] Published in the *News and Courier,* September 30, 1890.

fore, as a true Democrat," he said in summary, "I cannot vote for Mr. Tillman. Legally, I would not vote for him. From self-respect, I would not vote for him, and a ticket should be run against him." As a means through which victory might be won, he expressed his intention of appealing to the Negro vote. "When the white race divides," he said, "it is a question with the colored race which party will govern the State." However, he said that in case of success he would not give the Negroes offices, although he promised "government in the interest of both races." He claimed as precedent for this appeal the fact that the Hampton movement of 1876 had made a like appeal to the black voters. He closed with a call for a nominating convention to meet in Columbia.

The Haskell convention met on October 9 with twenty of the thirty-five counties represented by men of high position and choice names.[38a] With a great throng of prominent men and women in

[38a] The most notable of the 186 present were: Alfred Aldrich, of Barnwell; Porcher Smith, of Berkeley; J. W. Barnwell, of Charleston; J. J. Lucas and James Wilcox, of Darlington; Thomas Woodward, J. D. Harrison and G. W. Ragsdale, of Fairfield; W. W. Harllee, of Florence; W. H. Ancrum, James Cantey and A. H. and T. W. Boykin, of Kershaw; W. D. Johnson, A. T. Harllee, E. A. Bethea, of Marion; J. D. Peterkin and W. D. and D. H. Trezevant, of Orangeburg; R. W. Shand, R. S. Desportes, Richard Singleton, William Weston and Allen Green, of Richland; Edward Bacon and Samuel McGowan, Jr., of Spartanburg; Ellison D. Smith, J. C. Singleton, J. D. Blanding, W. T. Aycock and Henry Spann, of Sumter; John M. Jeter, W. C. Wallace, T. B. Butler and A. F. McKissick, of Union; and Iredell Jones, of York.

the galleries, the work of the assembly was accomplished in the short period of one hour and twenty minutes; it was the haste of conservative white South Carolinians conscious of performing the disagreeable duty of acting in opposition to a majority of their race. In order to give the proceedings conservative dignity, an attempt was made to clothe the work of the convention in the mantle of 1876. The red jacket which the Fairfield delegation had displayed at the previous convention was again in evidence; the chairman of the nominating convention of 1876 became the chairman of this one; Haskell himself had been one of the boldest champions of Hampton in 1876; and the new party created was called the Straight-Out Democracy, the name which the Hampton party had assumed in 1876. After the proposal that only a candidate for governor be nominated was rejected with derision, a full ticket with Haskell at its head was agreed upon and an address to the people adopted.

This address illustrates the passionate hatred which its authors cherished for Tillman. He was accused of having resorted to secret caucuses and class appeal in order to secure his nomination, of having caused a state of turbulence among the people which had prevented "decent and grave discussion," and of having driven ladies from the campaign meetings by the use of profane language. His speeches, it was affirmed, "have been of such a nature as to cause their condemnation by every man who respected the truths of religion." The conclusion was as follows:

> We further solemnly allege that B. R. Tillman . . . has done more harm and brought greater sorrow on the State than the sword or the hand of man in any other shape has effected. . . . We do pledge ourselves as men and citizens to war unceasingly against such unworthy men and methods as have so ruthlessly torn the heart of our State in twain, to feed upon it for personal gain.[39]

That portion of the anti-Tillmanites who had refused to send representation to this assembly gave the independent movement little open support. Although perhaps they felt as much contempt for Tillman as did the Haskellites, they were not willing to sacrifice white unity in order to follow a movement with such scant possibilities of success. "A ticket," said the *News and Courier,*[40] "might have been nominated in protest and dropped if Republican opposition developed." As Haskell was adjudged not to have followed this policy, this newspaper charged him for publicity and put Tillman's name at the head of its editorial column. "Captain Tillman," said a typical expression from the press,[41] "was not our choice for

[39] For the proceedings of the convention, see the *News and Courier* and Charleston *World,* October 10, 1890.

[40] *News and Courier,* October 11, 1890.

[41] *Lancaster Ledger,* October 8, 1890, quoted in the *News and Courier,* October 9, 1890.

Governor, but he was the choice of a large majority of the Democratic party. . . . Every Democrat is pledged in honor to vote for him." Only three newspapers[42] openly endorsed the Haskell movement. General Hampton signified his intention of voting for Tillman. Yet when asked to address a meeting organized in opposition to Haskell, he, although he was soon to become a candidate for reëlection to the United States Senate before a pro-Tillman legislature, said: "I shall not denounce the man [Haskell] who was my comrade in war . . . and my trusted friend in 1876."[43]

The Negroes manifested little enthusiasm for Haskell, who in return for their vote had promised only fair play without a share of the public offices. They remembered how extreme he had been in his denunciation of them in 1876 and observed how he attempted to revive the traditions of that year. Consequently a meeting of Richland County Negroes reminded Haskell of the fact that he had raided one of their meetings in 1876; a convention of Negro intellectuals advised the race to take no part in the canvass; and Richard Carroll, a rising leader of his race, said, "Tillman has done more good than any living man since the War." However, the executive committee of

[42] The *Sumter Watchman and Southron*, the *Darlington Herald*, and the *Palmetto Post*.

[43] Hampton to Irby, October 23, 1890.

the Republican party did endorse Haskell, giving as its reason the fact that Tillman desired to call a constitutional convention through which the blacks could be disfranchised and that Haskell favored a "free and fair vote." The masses of the blacks, either fearful of a return to the terroristic methods of the elections of 1876, 1878, and 1880, or else indifferent to political affairs, showed no interest in the approaching contest and made few attempts to vote on election day.[44]

The Tillman leaders, conscious of the support of a large majority of the voters, never regarded the Haskell movement as a menace to their success. Irby, however, as chairman of the executive committee of the Democratic party, with the future maintenance of white unity in mind, invited such anti-Tillman Democrats as recognized the validity of Tillman's nomination to speak at political rallies held in various parts of the state. Tillman, in commenting upon the Haskell movement, said:

> They left the party of their own accord, and my opinion, in the words of General Hampton,[45] is, "Such independents are worse than the vilest radicals." I tremble for the future . . . , for any man who attempts to lead the negroes of Edgefield to vote the independent ticket runs a great personal risk.[46]

[44] For reports of the activity of the Negroes, see the *News and Courier,* September 20; October 6, 1890.

[45] In 1876.

[46] *Columbia Evening Record,* October 10, 1890, quoted in *News and Courier,* October 11, 1890.

Tillman won the November election by a majority too overwhelming to have been achieved without the support of anti-Tillman Democrats. Nevertheless, many of the latter group voted against him, for Haskell carried Berkeley and Beaufort Counties and received more than twenty per cent. of the votes in twelve additional counties.[47] The legislature chosen at this same election was composed of a Tillman majority of one hundred on a joint ballot of the two houses. The great majority were farmers. However, due to the fact that most of the farmers had had no legislative experience, the leadership of the body naturally passed to the few lawyers among the Tillman partisans. These were Irby, who became speaker of the House, John L. McLaurin, and John Gary Evans.[48]

[47] The vote was Tillman, 59,159; Haskell, 14,828. *Reports and Resolutions,* 1890, I. 604.

[48] For biographical sketches of each of the 160 members of the legislature, see the *News and Courier,* November 20-21, 1890.

CHAPTER VI

TILLMAN'S FIRST ADMINISTRATION

On December 4, 1890, the largest crowd ever gathered in the plaza in front of the State Capitol assembled to witness the inauguration of Tillman as governor of South Carolina. Many were perched in trees or hanging on the surrounding monuments. It was the same picnic crowd which in the previous summer had, before fifty rural platforms, yelled "Hurrah for Tillman" and which had now come to witness the triumph of its idol. In the crowd and on the list of those specially invited to sit on the platform were few from Columbia and Charleston or of aristocratic names, such as were wont to grace the advent of a new governor. Likewise, remarked an observer, the man who arose to address the assembled multitude, after he had taken the oath of office, was different in looks and manner from the typical governor of South Carolina. In place of the long white or raven hair and pleasing and agile movements of the typical governor, were shortly cropped hair, a dark complexion, a certain uncanny blankness about the face caused by the empty left eye socket, a set expression not broken by a smile, a firm mouth, and an awkardness in movement. In repose he appeared to be just a common farmer on parade. The unusual qualities of the man that lay hidden beneath such a stolid external appearance were not revealed until he got into action. Then the sparkle of his single eye revealed the fire beneath; then the variations in his shrill voice and his clever gestures showed that he had strong feelings, and his hard words and broad generalizations, based on concrete facts and unblemished by a high style, proved that he knew the significance of the movement which he led and was ready to give it a program of procedure.[1]

He began with an attempt to explain the significance of the occasion:

> The citizens of this great commonwealth have, for the first time in its history, demanded and obtained for themselves the right to choose their Governor, and I, as leader and exponent of this revolution which has brought about this change, am here to enter upon the discharge of its onerous duties. With such an audience as this, I might, if I were an orator, attempt to win your sympathy by flights of what some call eloquence, but which sensible people consider "glittering generalities," the tinsel and brass buttons of a dress parade, meaning nothing and worth nothing. . . . The responsibilities of my position demand practical statesmanship. We are here to do business; not evolve beautiful theories or discuss ideal government. We come as reformers, claiming that many things in the government are wrong. Democracy has won

[1] Full accounts of the inauguration are in the *News and Courier*, and the Columbia *Daily Register*, December 5, 1890.

a great victory unparalleled. The triumph of Democracy and white supremacy over mongrelism and anarchy is most complete.

Then followed a frank explanation of the attitude he would assume toward the Negro. "The whites," he said, "have absolute control of the government and we intend, at any hazard, to retain it. The intelligent exercise of the right of suffrage is as yet beyond the capacity of the vast majority of colored men. We deny, without regard to color, that all men are created equal, it is not true now and was not true when Jefferson wrote it." Yet this bold confession of determination to pursue a policy at variance with the profession of South Carolina politicians, white and black, left room for something more than "glittering generalities" concerning the welfare of the Negro. Along with the assertion that there "never was any just reason why the white man and the black man of Carolina should not live together in peace" went a concrete remedy for the injustice done to Negroes by lawless whites. He asked that the governor be given the right to remove from office sheriffs who failed to prevent mob violence.

The larger portion of his address was concerned with the advocacy of concrete reforms in the public administration. For the improvement of public education, he advocated making the rural school districts more compact, the increase to three dollars of the constitutional poll tax for the benefit of the common schools, the abolition of the "grand University" and the establishment in its place of a college of liberal arts, and the transference of the appliances of its mechanical and agricultural department to Clemson College. He favored the appointment of a commission to investigate the advisability of the establishment of a girls' industrial school. While he was of the opinion that the reopening of the South Carolina Military Academy after Reconstruction had been unwise, he was willing to continue its existence as a "landmark of the old régime."

The other reforms which he advocated were certain changes in the administration of the Lunatic Asylum, the re-apportionment of legislative representation, the abolition of one of Charleston's two senatorships, and the centralization of the tax administration so as to evolve a more just system of assessments. To justify the necessity of the latter reform, he cited figures to prove that banks had been guilty of tax evasion. To eliminate the "undue influence" of railroads, he asked that the railroad commission be reorganized and "honest men" put in charge of it. In addition, he asked the reorganization of township government.

At great length, he advanced his ideas of the disposition that should be made of the state's rights in the phosphate deposits when the contract, which had been granted to a corporation under acts of 1870 and 1876, to mine these deposits in return for a royalty of one dollar on each ton should expire on March 1, 1891. Tillman claimed that the stockholders of the company had become inordinately rich under this lease. He demanded that a survey be made to determine the value of the deposits and that in the meantime the royalty be raised to two dollars a ton.[2]

This address received the enthusiastic applause of the Governor's friends and the universal respect of his enemies. To say that it was the ablest and most significant official utterance of any South Carolinian since 1861 is faint praise beside that which his opponents gave it at the time it was delivered. Said one of these: "We cannot help saying that this inaugural address is perhaps the strongest state paper we have ever read. . . . A man who can think and labor as B. R. Tillman must have done on this address, must be a man of phenomenal force."[3]

In accordance with the Governor's wish, a bill designed to give him authority to remove sheriffs failing to protect Negroes against mobs was introduced. But it failed of passage in the sessions of both 1890 and 1891, because the anti-Tillman minority were able to convince a majority that the

[2] Inaugural Address, *House Journal,* 1890, pp. 131-154.

[3] James T. Bacon in *Edgefield Chronicle,* December 9, 1890.

purpose of the bill was to gratify the Chief Executive's lust for more power.[4] In spite of this failure to see enacted a means whereby lynching might be prevented, the first year of Tillman's administration was not disgraced by a single lynching, which was a pleasant contrast to twelve such occurences in one year (1889) of the previous administration. That there was a connection between this fact and his vigorous expression of intentions can hardly be doubted. When the first of the six lynchings during the second year of his administration did occur, that of Lundy who had murdered the son of the sheriff of Edgefield, he was vigorous in his denunciation of that official for alleged neglect of duty, although the latter was a personal friend.[5] He attributed the five additional lynchings to the refusal of the legislature to give him more power.[6]

In keeping with Tillman's belief that the Negro should be more adequately subordinated than had previously been the case, several bills were introduced. The first of these would have compelled separate railroad coaches for the two races. Over the protest of the colored members from Beaufort and of the railroad interests, the bill passed the House by a great majority, but failed to get a

[4] *House Journal,* 1891, p. 365.

[5] *News and Courier,* December 10, 16, 1890.

[6] For a list of lynchings in the state, see the National Association for the Advancement of Colored People, *Thirty Years of Lynching in United States,* p. 88.

favorable consideration from the Senate.[7] The growing sentiment for racial segregation had not as yet been sufficiently developed. Likewise, the oft-repeated demand of Tillman that a constitutional convention be called whereby the Negro might be more effectively disfranchised failed to get the necessary two thirds vote from the House, although it did pass the Senate.[8] Moreover, the demand of the Governor that the system of determining congressional districts, by which the greater portion of the Negro political strength was concentrated in one district, be abolished met with failure at the hands of a legislature reluctant to interfere with the established relations with the Negro.[9] The ostensible purpose of the Governor was to prevent the state being "held up to scorn before the nation for the construction of a district the like of which had never been seen before;" his real motive was to distribute Negro power in such a way as to prevent the return of even one black congressman. The only successful attempt of the first administration to restrict the liberty of the black man was the imposition of a prohibitive tax upon the operation of labor agents who were in the habit of inducing the emigration of black farm hands.[10]

[7] *House Journal,* 1891, p. 276; *News and Courier,* December 22, 1890.

[8] *House Journal,* 1891, p. 281; *Senate Journal,* 1891, p. 103.

[9] *Senate Journal,* 1891, p. 34.

[10] *Acts and Joint Resolutions,* 1891, p. 1084.

Following the recommendation of Tillman, the legislature radically altered the status of the University of South Carolina. Its agricultural and mechanical departments were abolished, and its trustees were divested of their authority over the military college and Claflin College for Negroes. A new board of trustees, composed of the governor, several other state officials, and nine members elected by the legislature, was authorized to reorganize the university into a college of "theoretical science, law, literature and art." The academic staff was reduced from twenty-five to thirteen.[11] During the inquiry necessary to determine which professors should be dismissed, Tillman questioned Professor W. J. Alexander, a Unitarian, who was a professor of philosophy, concerning the latter's attitude toward the divinity of Christ. No affirmative answer of a nature pleasing to the orthodox was forthcoming. Alexander's name later appeared among those dropped from the college's list. This led to the charge that Tillman was guilty of an invasion of the right of freedom of academic thought, a charge apparently sustained by his words to the dismissed professor.[12]

[11] *Acts and Joint Resolutions,* 1890, pp. 687-91; *Reports and Resolutions,* 1891, I. 328-30.

[12] "There is a vast difference", said Tillman in a letter to Alexander, May 20, 1891, "between allowing his dogmas to be taught in public schools and allowing him to profess them." Tillman Scrapbook, No. 4.

Perhaps nothing has come nearer discrediting Tillman with later generations of South Carolinians than the charge that he restricted the functions of the university in order to gratify personal venom. One cannot deny that Tillman, a man of strong feelings, did cherish resentment against the institution whose benefits he had not received, which nurtured his enemies, whose students had mocked him,[13] and whose pretensions stood in the way of the development of his cherished ideas of agricultural education. However, he did not wish to destroy the university to advance the type of education in which he was most interested, for he had a high respect for a literary education, even when conducted by those for whom he had no love. There can be no doubt that the reforms he instituted in the organization of the college were salutary. The usual annual appropriation of $30,000 was not reduced until two years later, and then as a part of the program in the general reduction of public appropriations, and the reduced revenue of the college was sufficient to maintain it in a state of efficiency at least equal to that which had existed before 1890, in view of the fact that expenses were lowered through the reduction of

[13] The students had hissed him at the March convention and followed him to his hotel, singing "Hang Ben Tillman on a sour apple tree." Charleston *World,* March 28, 1890. "This procedure," said Tillman, in a speech at Anderson, "has soured me." Charleston *World,* May 12, 1890.

a faculty which had been obviously too numerous for a student body of less than two hundred.[14]

We have no reason to believe that Professor Alexander would have been retained had he been most orthodox in his opinions, although the fact that he was questioned on matters of faith lent color to the charge that an issue of academic freedom was involved, and no doubt the orthodox majority got satisfaction from the dismissal of one holding questionable views. Under the plan for the reorganization of the college, half of the faculty was slated for dismissal, and Alexander was among that number. Tillman's mistake was in allowing religious questions to arise. As one who had been criticized for his own indifference toward religion, he was not the one to create a religious issue and was frank in his personal sympathy for Alexander.[15]

The Governor showed greater moderation in dealing with the military academy, which he had derisively designated as a "dude factory." Although he was pledged to the necessity of asking support for two new industrial colleges, and felt

[14] The university had 226 students in 1890; 182 in 1891. Edward L. Green, *History of the University of South Carolina*, p. 438.

[15] In a private letter to Professor Alexander, April 22, 1891, he said: "The seeker after truth, the man who in this vale of tears tries to do what is right without pandering to the prejudices of the multitude must expect persecution and sorrow as his lot. To the few is given the ability to swim against the current of popular ideas. The masses inherit their religion." Tillman Scrapbook, No. 4.

that the state would never again have the nationalistic aspirations which had prompted the creation before the Civil War of an academy strictly devoted to military training, he did not tamper with the organization of that institution's governing board or dismiss any of its faculty.

In addition to legislation furthering the construction of Clemson College, Governor Tillman, in his first administration, did much to promote industrial education for the young white women of the state. In 1883 the school board of the city of Columbia had called David B. Johnson, a young educator from Tennessee, to organize a normal school for women. With the aid of funds from the Peabody Board of Massachusetts, secured by Johnson through the aid of Robert C. Winthrop, the Winthrop Training School was opened in Columbia, November 15, 1886, with Johnson and three women teachers in charge and with twenty-one pupils in attendance. Before the Farmers' Convention of 1886 Tillman had said: "The State owes to its daughters a school where they can be taught not only to adorn a drawing room, but be fitted to perform the duties of life and become breadwinners." These words were followed in 1887 by a state appropriation of one scholarship from each county, valued at $150 each, for students to attend Winthrop Training School. At the suggestion of Professor Erward S. Joynes of the university, Tillman spoke in his inaugural message of "the imperative need of a [new] industrial school for girls." Following this suggestion, the legislature appointed, in 1890, a commission composed of Johnson and two women educational experts to visit institutions in other states in order to prepare plans for a South Carolina normal college. The report of this commission bore fruit in the act of 1891 providing for the establishment of "a first-class institution for the thorough education of the white girls of South Carolina in the practice of teaching, cooking, dress-making," etc. After bids from various towns in the state for the location of the institution in their midst, the contract was awarded to Rock Hill, a progressive town in the county of York. Under the supervision of Johnson, who was to become president of the institution, and Governor Tillman, who was its leading trustee, and by the use of the liberal subsidies of Rock Hill, the moderate appropriations of the legislature, and Negro convict labor, handsome buildings were constructed, and Winthrop Normal and Industrial College was able to open its doors, October 15, 1895, with 304 students.[16]

Much ill feeling came from Tillman's resolve to reform the administration of the South Caro-

[16] Adequate treatments of the early history of Winthrop College are: Edward S. Joynes, *Origin and Early History of Winthrop,* and Ira B. Jones, *Corner Stone Address,* May 12, 1894.

lina Lunatic Asylum. The reduction of the number of regents from nine to five caused resignations from that board in protest, and the giving to the governor of the right to fill vacancies provoked much criticism. On the initiative of the Governor, an investigation of the administration of the institution, growing out of the belief that there had been irregularities, was held. Although much bitterness was engendered, no proof of any charge was established except that of carelessness. On the basis of the latter charge the Governor summarily dismissed the superintendent, appointing in his place, J. W. Babcock, a Harvard graduate, who later became a national authority on nervous diseases and pellagra and who gave the institution a very efficient administration for twenty years.[17]

Acting on the advice of Governor Tillman, the legislature reapportioned the 124 seats of the House of Representatives according to the census of 1890. This resulted in the reduction of the representation of Charleston from twelve to eight and that of several counties of the low-country by one, all to the advantage of the up-country.[18]

As the Governor had asked, the royalty on phosphate mining was increased from one to two dollars and a commission, with himself as chair-

[17] For the controversy over the administration of the asylum, see the *News and Courier, passim,* April to June, 1891.

[18] *Acts and Joint Resolutions,* 1891, p. 1070.

man, was created with the authority to take charge of the industry and to survey the deposits. Accordingly, the commission took possession and issued licenses for three companies of its own choice to carry on operations. But this plan was interrupted when the company which had previously operated the mines obtained an order from the United States circuit court enjoining the new companies from operations. When, after much litigation, the courts finally allowed, in March, 1892, the licensees of the state to begin operations, the state had lost, due to the closing of the mines, some $68,000 in revenue and had given the newly-discovered mines of Florida opportunity to gain in the competition. The commission failed to secure a survey of the deposits, as the appropriation provided for that purpose was inadequate.

Although the state was successful in its efforts to increase the royalty, only for one year was the total amount of revenue derived equal to the average of the previous ten years; after 1893 a rapid decline of the revenue set in, due to the Florida competition. While it is most likely that the phosphate interests of the state would have suffered in competition with the deposits of Florida regardless of what action may have been taken, there can be little doubt that the interference of the South Carolina agrarian governor in a matter of which he had little understanding served to hasten this process. When questioned concerning his indictment of the previous administration of the state's interests in the mines, Tillman said, "I did a good deal of blowing last summer."[19]

One of the most prolonged struggles of the first administration grew out of Tillman's desire to reorganize the railroad commission in keeping with his personal opinions. A bill was introduced giving the governor the right to appoint and suspend members of the commission and giving the commission authority to fix "fair and reasonable" rates without the right of appeal to the court.[20]

The legislature, however, objected to giving the governor the right of appointment and dismissal, and the companies objected to being denied the right of appeal from the decisions of the commission. The result was that the bill, which passed both houses, provided for the election of the commission by the legislature and did not deny the right of judicial review. The Governor, angered at what he considered a personal affront and an undue deference to the courts, vetoed the bill at the close of the session of 1890.[21] The bill failed again at the session of 1891, because the

[19] For these facts, see legislative investigation, *Reports and Resolutions,* 1892, I. 235-250. For the history of the decline of the state's phosphate mining, see annual Reports of the Phosphate Commission in *Reports and Resolutions, passim,* 1890-1900.

[20] See Columbia *Daily Register,* December 13, 1890, for the text of bill.

[21] *House Journal,* 1890, p. 272.

Governor and Senate could not agree as to the manner of election.[22]

Likewise, the legislature failed in the oft-repeated recommendation that the public expenditures be reduced. This was impracticable at the time, owing to the fact that the carrying out of the reforms attempted by the Tillman administration necessitated some actual increases in expenditures and that the government under the Hampton influence had been conducted at near the minimum cost. There had been little or no increased expense, and the budgets of the state institutions and the salaries of public officials were already pitifully small. Consequently Tillman and his legislature had to content themselves with minor savings. The contingent funds of certain state officials were reduced; the completion of Clemson College was delayed by a refusal to grant an extra appropriation; a subsidy was withheld from the state fair; and no appropriation was made for a South Carolina exhibit at the World's Fair at Chicago. As it was, the total expenditures of neither of the first two years of the Tillman administration were as low as the average of a ten year period of the previous conservative government.[23]

[22] *News and Courier,* January 2, 1892.

[23] Under Republican rule (1868-1876), the average annual expenditure of the state was $1,886,000. For a ten year period of conservative rule (1877-1887), this average was $1,026,000. In

The Governor, however, was more successful in his efforts to shift some of the burden of taxation from land to corporations. He began his efforts in this direction by publishing in detail the proof that certain named corporations were not bearing their just share of the tax burden. The result was that the assessed value of the property of the state was raised from $150,000,000 to $168,000,000. More than fifty per cent. of the increase was upon corporate wealth.[24] This was regarded as a salutary reform, tending to put upon the shoulders of the most profitable form of wealth a fairer proportion of the tax burden.

Giving most satisfaction to the Tillman partisans and causing most dissatisfaction to the Governor's opponents, was the election of Tillmanites to such offices as became vacant. Irby became speaker of the House of Representatives, McLaurin, attorney general and Y. J. Pope, a justice of the Supreme Court. Very disconcerting to conservatives was the defeat of William Wallace, their candidate for the latter position. Wallace had been speaker of the famous "Wallace House" of 1876[25] and had long been a circuit judge. However, he had incurred the anger of Tillman,

1890 the total expenditure was $1,112,000. During the first year of Tillman's administration the total was $1,151,000; during his second year, $1,125,000. Compilation by the author from *Reports and Resolutions,* 1869-1893.

[24] Report of the State Treasurer, *Reports and Resolutions,* 1891, II. 310.

[25] That is, the Democratic faction of the House of that year.

because he had ordered an election official of Charleston County to return the books of his office to the official's predecessor, whom Tillman had deposed on the ground that his appointment had not been confirmed by the Senate.[26] The defeat of Wallace[27] was interpreted as an instance of improper interference of the executive with judicial processes and as an example of a noble leader of the past becoming the victim of an up-start tyrant.

The act of Tillman's first term most displeasing to the conservatives was the defeat of Hampton for reëlection to the United States Senate by the legislature in 1890. As soon as the complete triumph of the Tillman party became known, the conservatives began to plead that their adored chief be returned. The memories of 1861 and 1876 were recalled, and Generals Butler and Hagood begged that their old comrade in arms be spared. "Blot Wade Hampton from the history of the State for the past thirty years," said the *News and Courier*,[28] "and you blot out South Carolina." But Tillman remained obdurate. He recalled his experience at the Columbia meeting of the previous summer and an alleged personal

[26] Tillman's round denunciation of Wallace appears in his annual message to the legislature of 1891, *Senate Journal*, 1891, p. 25. The account of the points of difference between the two is in the Report of the Attorney General, *Reports and Resolutions*, 1892, I. 241.

[27] *House Journal*, 1891, p. 171.

[28] December 8, 1890.

slight which Hampton had visited upon him at Aiken. "If our Senator is not elected," he concluded, "he can attribute his defeat to his own acts."[29] Although the defeat of Hampton appeared as a foregone conclusion, his friends continued their protests to the moment of defeat. "God grant," said a senator from Charleston who had been denied the right of making a nomination speech, "that some revolution will hurl from power those who forget their duty to Wade Hampton." "The people of South Carolina," said another senator, "by the defeat of Wade Hampton will ruin their own State."[30] But Hampton's defeat came by an overwhelming majority, since only a very few Tillman members of the legislature voted for him.[31]

The man elected to Hampton's place was Irby, the thirty-six-year-old leader of the Tillman political organization. He achieved his position because of a genial and commanding personality and his powers of political organization. His record should have made the Tillman leaders see the error of elevating him to the United States Senate. True to his past, he did nothing creditable during his six years in that body.

[29] *News and Courier*, December 6, 1890.

[30] The procedure of the day is in the *News and Courier*, December 11, 1890.

[31] *House Journal*, 1890, p. 136.

Tillman's and Gary's criticism that the clique which surrounded Hampton controlled the public offices of the state for the selfish benefit of themselves and their friends, made at a time when neither Tillman nor Gary had public office within their grasp, can with equal justice be made by the critic of after times against the clique which surrounded Tillman. By methods more thorough than those of the easy-going Hampton, they took the public spoils for themselves. Tillman, once in public office, was never willing to make room for another and was content for two other members of his family to hold office at the same time he did. Four members of the Gary family,[32] all lawyers, were elected to office, and Hugh Farley, who had been an intimate friend of Martin Gary, was made adjutant general. Y. J. Pope was made a justice of the Supreme Court and his brother, who had been a schoolmate of Tillman, became clerk of the Senate. Lawyers, as formerly, continued to receive a large proportion of the public offices. While it is true that new men came into office, they were not the "wool-hat boys" and other poor men who made up the rank and file of Tillman's supporters.

How much of his program, as described in his inaugural message and in previous statements of

[32] Eugene B. Gary, Frank Gary, Ernest Gary, and John Gary Evans, all men of character and ability.

politics, had Tillman accomplished with the aid of his legislature after two years in office? The construction of Winthrop and Clemson Colleges had been advanced and South Carolina College reorganized; he had had his way in dealing with the phosphate interests and the Lunatic Asylum and in the election of the men whom he desired for the public offices which had become vacant. Legislative representation had been reapportioned; the assessment of the value of corporate wealth had been increased, and an anti-emigrant agent law[33] passed. Taking into consideration the fact that the majority of members of the legislature were men of no previous experience as lawmakers and the fact that precedent decreed that the sessions should not last longer than a month each,[34] we may well say that much was accomplished. The reason was that Tillman did not hesitate to use strong methods in his efforts to force the majority to do his bidding. In John Gary Evans and Irby he had two very effective floor leaders. On occasion, he used strong language in his characterization of refractory administration members and did not hesitate to call them to his office one by one and command them to change their votes.[35] But

[33] That is, a law imposing a very heavy license tax upon those engaged in recruiting labor for service outside of the state.

[34] This practice had come into existence as a reaction from the tendency of the Reconstruction legislatures to hold sessions of undue length.

[35] He called them "Damn fools" on one occasion. *News and Courier*, December 25, 1891. My authority for the attitude of the

such harsh methods had their limitation, even though the members were well aware that his anger would mean their defeat at the hands of constituencies pliant to his will. While there were many who in secret despised him but who did as he commanded them in order to keep their seats, a large number joined the conservatives in voting in opposition to him because of his rudeness and dictatorial tendencies. The result was that Tillman failed in his efforts to have enacted his railroad regulation bill, the bill allowing him to remove sheriffs, the bill for the reform of congressional districts, and the resolution for the calling of a constitutional convention. The first of these two bills failed because a majority of the legislature, feeling personal resentment towards the Governor, were determined not to give him increased powers of appointment. In addition, the majority rebuked him more straightforwardly on another issue: When the fact that the Governor had accepted a free pass upon the railroads of the state became known, a law was passed prohibiting public officials from receiving such favors.[36]

Governor towards the members is Reverend P. P. Blalock, then chaplain of the Senate.

[36] *Acts and Joint Resolutions,* 1891, p. 1047. The Governor had, without any attempt at secrecy, accepted the free pass on condition that the railroad company ask no favor of him. He was always desirous of saving what he could for himself.

The reaction of Tillman to personal snubs from the men whose political fortunes he had made was characteristic. In less than a week after the adjournment of the second session of the legislature, he, in response to a group of serenaders who visited him while he was enjoying the Christmas holidays with Irby at Laurens, denounced the members of the late legislature as "driftwood which the tidal wave of Tillmanism has swept into the Capitol." He now asked the people to give him a new legislature and a second term in which to complete his program of reform.[37]

[37] *News and Courier,* December 30, 1891.

CHAPTER VII

TILLMAN'S RE-ELECTION AND SECOND ADMINISTRATION

The announcement that Tillman would be a candidate for reëlection was followed by the adoption of measures by the anti-Tillmanites intended to checkmate his ambition. Although such moderate critics of Tillman as the Augusta *Chronicle* were of the opinion that his reëlection could not be prevented, and although Earle said, "Governor Tillman is as strong to-day as he ever was,"[1] his opponents were in no humor to surrender without a struggle. They were united by a dynamic hatred, even greater than that of 1890, for the man who had caused the defeat of Wallace and Hampton, who had effected certain agrarian and fiscal reforms, and who, when faced with the responsibilities of office, had not moderated the excessive rudeness of manner which had characterized his earlier agitations. They had on their side certain deserters from the Tillman cause and the wisdom gleaned from their experiences in 1890.

[1] Earle's Statements in the *News and Courier,* February 24-25, 1892.

In this spirit an assembly, called the Peace and Harmony convention, met in Columbia, March 24, 1892, with representatives from every county except Berkeley. Most conspicuous of the many notable conservatives present were Hampton, ex-Governors Sheppard and Richardson, and State Senator Laurence Youmans. While the Tillman administration was condemned, the convention pledged itself to abide by the verdict of the Democratic party and resolved not to "stir passions by general accusation which we [the anti-Tillmanites] cannot prove." Sheppard, a man of moderation, sounded the keynote, when he said it was necessary to "fight for the safety of South Carolina and for the elimination of a Governor who usurps the functions of the judiciary." After James L. Orr, a capitalist, had refused to accept the nomination for governor, that nomination was given to Sheppard. His aids in the forensic battle of the coming summer were Orr, candidate for lieutenant governor, and Youmans, candidate for secretary of state.[2]

The conservatives were less fortunate in their selections than they had been in 1890. Although Sheppard was admirably fitted to be governor of the state—he was a man of honor, had had a wide experience as a public servant and was a gifted orator of the old school—he was not capable of

[2] *News and Courier,* and Columbia *Daily Register,* March 24-26, 1892.

conducting with success a canvass on the plane which Tillman prescribed. He lacked personal magnetism, was somewhat uncertain as to his ground, and was too dignified to evoke the sympathy of crowds accustomed to the jolly banter of Tillman. His lack of humor and his stately manners made him the victim of the jests of Tillman and the crowds. Furthermore, the fact that he was both banker and lawyer gave the Tillman editors opportunity to brand him as the enemy of the class-conscious farmers. Yet he proved himself of sufficient stamina to withstand hostile audiences. The qualities which Sheppard lacked were supposed to be supplied by his aids, Orr and Youmans. The great physical strength and personal bravery of the former were designed to frighten Tillman, who, however, could not be frightened. Youmans was "a mustachioed strutter," too much in earnest and devoid of humor.[3]

In opposition to this combination, the Tillmanites marshalled their forces. The pro-Tillman Democratic executive committee, in session early in January, prescribed that those who had bolted the party in 1890 could only vote in the primary for the election of delegates to the nominating convention on the condition that they take an oath

[3] The author has been aided in the estimates of this paragraph by George R. Koester, *Greenville Piedmont,* October 19, 1916. Koester was the Columbia *Daily Register's* reporter in 1892.

J. C. SHEPPARD

to support loyally the party and its nominees. Negroes, who had been allowed to vote in the Democratic primary because of their loyalty to Hampton in 1876, were only to be allowed to vote when they could get ten white men to vouch for their loyalty.[4] When the conservatives made a request that the system of the direct primary for the nomination of state officials be substituted for the convention system, Chairman Irby, now that his faction was in control of the party, refused the request, saying that such a change would be unfair to the counties of the low-country, where the white vote was small.[5] John L. McLaurin was chosen as candidate for attorney general, so that he might aid Tillman in the coming forensic battle.

Two new forces in the form of pro-Tillman and anti-Tillman newspapers, edited by men of aggressive personalities, were destined to play a prominent part in the approaching canvass. On the demise of the *Charleston World,* with whose management he had quarreled, Tillman was without a daily newspaper champion. To fill this need, the Columbia *Daily Register* was purchased, promised the patronage of the public printing, and given as its editor T. Larry Gantt, who had made a reputation in Georgia as a partisan of the Farmers' Alliance. Endowed with all the preju-

[4] *News and Courier,* January 6, 1892.

[5] *Ibid.,* January 26, 1892.

dices and doctrines of the agrarian agitators of his day, possessed of a spirited and direct style, violently partisan, but never bitter, Gantt was the very man to supplement Tillman's efforts to arouse the farmers against the townsmen. He did not hesitate to parade the private affairs of the opposition before the public or to give the most dignified gentlemen ridiculous nicknames. When threatened with violence if he did not leave the state, by those who resented such violent language from a newly-arrived citizen, he showed courage. "If I leave South Carolina," he said,[5a] "before my mission is ended, it will be in a casket with feet foremost." The rival of Gantt's newspaper was the Columbia *State,* first issued on February 8, 1891, by N. G. Gonzales, who had left his position as Columbia correspondent of the *News and Courier* in order to carry on a truceless warfare against Tillman unrestrained by the conservatism of the Charleston newspaper. Although he was the most brilliant and forceful editor that South Carolina has produced since the death of Dawson in 1889, and although he is chiefly responsible for the fact that the *State* exists today as the most powerful newspaper of South Carolina, he was as much, or more, a factor in the defeat of the cause which he championed as was his opponent Gantt. He tactlessly offended many

[5a] Columbia *Daily Register,* April 10, 1892.

and was without Gantt's humor; he manifested little understanding of the manner in which the voters might be won from the hated Tillman; by raising issues, he gave Tillman full opportunity to use his great talent for striking back.

Before an audience of 5000, at Greenville, April 16, at the first meeting of the campaign, Tillman, by the use of bitter ridicule and humor, demonstrated his superiority to Sheppard and Orr with whom he debated. "I am here," he began amidst the plaudits of the crowd, "to meet my traducers face to face, and let God and justice stand between us." He made the most of the issue between the farmer and business man, saying: "The issue is, whether the people or the corporations will govern." Amidst derisive laughter, he attacked the "Peace and Harmony" policy of his enemies. The only reason, he said, that there would be no bolt from the party in 1892 was because "the enemy had tried the negro and failed." He defined the Columbia *State* as the "organ founded by the Haskellites to keep alive prejudice and malice." A hand primary revealed a great majority in his favor, and both his ridicule of his opponents and his defense of himself brought to life the friendly laughs and howls of 1890. Aroused by certain charges which Sheppard and Orr had made against him and angered by howls only less rude than those with which his partisans had annoyed his opponents, Tillman, in rebuttal, spoke with fierceness. In answer to Sheppard's assertion that he (Sheppard) would carry both men's home county of Edgefield, he said: "I will go home, and if I can't win in the primaries I will withdraw from the race. . . . I have gone through hell to become Governor, and have been told that no other man could make this movement a success." "I had rather follow the majority to hell," he said in attempting to express his aversion for his adversaries, "than these men to heaven." Deeply offended because Orr had said that he was "not fit to unlatch the shoes of Judge Wallace," he accused Orr of being "the president of a factory that is making poor men and women work thirteen hours a day." He was most extreme in his characterization of the "driftwood" legislature. It had been "bamboozled and controlled by demagogues;" he would make the candidates for the next legislature swear on Bibles that they would support him.[6]

After debating throughout many counties of the up-country in the same manner as at Greenville, Tillman went to Edgefield to ask his home people for vindication from the charges made against his character. He said:

> I have a rough outside; God did not make me of silken material to bamboozle men, to give lip service or to pre-

[6] Columbia *Daily Register,* Columbia *State,* and *News and Courier,* April 17-18, 1892.

tend what I do not mean; but my heart beats warm for the people of South Carolina and those who know me best love me most. Although I make no pretensions to religion or to being a churchman, is there a man here who ever knew me to do an act of dishonor or dishonesty?[7]

The probability that the joint debates might lead to serious trouble increased as the canvass progressed. Neither Tillman nor Orr and Youmans would let up in their violent characterizations of their opponents, and the crowds, excited by the speakers, became more and more menacing. Certain drunken members of the crowd at Walterboro were so noisy and profane in their speech that no speaker was able to get an uninterrupted hearing. For two hours Youmans vainly attempted to be heard. "The conduct of the rowdies," said an observer,[8] "was such as would have been a reproach to a negro bedlam." The conduct of neither Tillman nor his opponents at Charleston was such as to allay the excited feelings of the masses. The *News and Courier* had said:

His speech would be a trying ordeal for self-respecting Charlestonians. He makes no attempt to being a gentleman. He scorns refinement of manner and speech and prefers "damn you" to "if you please."[9]

Tillman, the next day, before a hostile audience, spoke in the manner of his 1888 speech. The editor who had denied him the title of gentleman,

[7] *News and Courier,* May 4, 1892.
[8] Koester in the Columbia *Daily Register,* June 14, 1892.
[9] June 14, 1892.

he said, was "an up-country ragamuffin who used to go around in copperas breeches," and his newspaper was accused of giving the speaker an aristocratic pedigree at the time of his inauguration in order to win him to its side.[10] The intense feeling of the canvass reached climaxes at Florence on June 30 and at Edgefield a week later. At the former place the trouble was precipitated when a delegation from the nearby village of Timmonsville brought forward a banner graphically representing Tillman as "the Great Bamboozler running away from our Youmanry," which a giant member of the delegation hoisted above the speakers' stand. After the bearer refused to remove the emblem, the Tillmanites rushed toward the platform with drawn pistols. What might have been bloodshed was prevented by Youmans' effective insistence that the cause of the trouble be removed. This was followed by an attempt made by Youmans to force Tillman to recant a previous assertion that "Earle was a more honorable man than Youmans." Tillman's reply was, "Not a damn bit." When a minister of the town tried to make him apologize for the use of the word *damn,* he refused to do so amidst a scene of menacing disorder.[11] At Edgefield, where the

[10] In 1890 the *News and Courier* had published a biographical sketch asserting, perhaps through the ignorance of the writer, that Tillman was descended from the aristocratic Maryland family of Tilghman.

[11] Account in the *News and Courier,* June 15, 1982.

speakers had gone for a return engagement, trouble grew out of the fact that the audience would not allow Youmans to be heard because of his previous violent language against Tillman. When McLaurin arose to speak he was met with retaliatory shouts, and a determined Sheppard partisan sent the proposed speaker word that if he attempted to speak there would be violence. In order to prevent possible bloodshed, Tillman suggested adjournment. After this was accomplished, the Tillman partisans bore him and McLaurin to the piazza of the nearby village academy, where they prepared to speak. Angered by this defeat of their purpose, the anti-Tillmanites advanced in mass formation upon the Tillmanites. A pitched battle seemed imminent, but was prevented by the retreat of the Tillmanites to the court house with McLaurin and Tillman on their shoulders. Behind a guard of posted sentinels, who only admitted Tillmanites, both Tillman and McLaurin were given opportunity to speak.[12]

Such wild conduct as had characterized the Walterboro, Charleston, Florence, and Edgefield meetings was only once repeated at the remaining meetings of the canvass. The authorities of the towns, alarmed at what might happen, closed the saloons; the populace saw the folly of preventing

[12] For the Edgefield meeting, see George R. Koester, Columbia *Daily Register,* July 8, 1892, and *Greenville Piedmont,* October 14, 1916; *News and Courier,* July 8, 1892.

the opposition candidates from speaking when such conduct was bound to be followed with like conduct on the part of the opposition; the candidates themselves learned to conduct themselves with more equinamity. Near violence, however, did come at Union, when the giant Orr said that all the ministers of the state were against Tillman because the latter cursed and boasted of not going to church. "I do curse sometimes," said Tillman frankly, "but there is not a drop of the hypocrite in me. . . . Any preacher or anybody else who says that I boasted of not going to church lies." Face to face, the two men came near fighting, while the crowd, with pistols ready, massed on the platform. Orr did not strike. "If Orr had laid his burly hands on Tillman," said the correspondent of the *Register,* "there would not have been enough left of his huge body to bury."[13]

The county-to-county canvass of 1892 was a spectacle most disappointing to those who imagined that by such a method the issues between the candidates could be brought before the people. Instead of a calm discussion of differences of opinion, through which plain men might arrive at intelligent decisions as to how to cast their ballots, there was a resort to personalities, groundless accusations, and true accusations of such a private nature as to be unbecoming in men who were

[13] Columbia *Daily Register* and *State,* August 26, 1892.

candidates for responsible public offices. The crowds, instead of listening to the arguments of the men whom they had selected as their candidates for public office, spent most of their time yelling for their favorites and against those whom they did not like. There can be little doubt that Tillman, as the individual who had organized public opinion and as the man who profited most from these disturbances, was largely responsible for the ugly moods of the crowds and the speakers. He knew that his previous success had been largely due to his power to arouse angry opposition and a more than counteracting sympathy for himself on the part of the agricultural majority. He made violent accusations against the public and private conduct of his opponents; he arrayed the rural majority against the business men and aristocrats of the towns.[14] However, his opponents should not be wholly acquitted of responsibility for this unseemly canvass. Being aware that there was no chance of defeating Tillman by the ordinary methods of politics, they resorted to extreme methods. Orr and Youmans deliberately attempted to bully Tillman by a display of their undoubted courage and by threats of physical force. They tried to discredit him

[14] Dr. C. P. DeVore, a planter of Edgefield and close friend of Tillman, tells this story: "Ben," said DeVore to Tillman, "why do you raise so much hell?" "Well", replied Tillman, "if I didn't, the damn fools wouldn't vote for me."

personally, accusing him of irreligion and blasphemy. Aside from the question of civic morality, there was much to admire in the manner in which Tillman conducted the canvass. He refused to be bullied and outdid his enemies at the game of demagoguery.

As was expected, the result of the primary of August 29, held for the election of delegates to the nominating convention, was an overwhelming victory for Tillman and for those candidates who saw the wisdom of calling him their "political daddy." He received a majority of 22,000 out of a total popular vote of 87,000. The Sheppard ticket carried only five of the thirty-five counties. Tillman carried Edgefield by a majority of 1400. Five of the seven congressmen elected were Tillmanites. The people had obeyed in a thorough fashion his injunction "to kill off the race of fence straddlers" by giving him a new assembly to supplant the "driftwood" legislature. Only eight of the thirty-six senators and twenty-two of the 124 representatives returned were anti-Tillmanites. Of the 102 Tillmanites of the new House, only twenty-seven had sat in the old, and most of these had records satisfactory to Tillman. The vast majority were new men, ready to do what their "political daddy," acting through Cole L. Blease as House leader and John Gary Evans as Senatorial leader, would have them. Most of the county officials elected had as their chief title to public esteem the fact that they were friends of "Ole Ben."[15] Tillman could now begin his second term with more power and a more pronounced popular mandate than he had had in 1890.

One of those who was a victim of the determination of the Tillmanites to rid the state of all public servants who did not favor the Tillman program was Tillman's brother, George, who was defeated for reëlection to Congress by Jasper Talbert. George was defeated because he cherished a whimsical aversion to the secret political methods of the Farmers' Alliance and that organization's national platform, which was adopted at a convention held at Ocala, Florida, to which the Tillmanites had committed themselves. "We can't give Uncle George our support," said the official organ of Tillman,[16] "because he doesn't stand on the Ocala platform." Although Ben Tillman personally disliked Talbert, he did nothing to save his brother from the wrath of his agrarian followers. In fact the two brothers had become estranged in 1890, when Ben, cherishing the desire to be United States senator after he had served two terms as governor, frustrated George's ambition to succeed Hampton in the Senate. The younger brother felt that his own chances would

[15] For election results, see the *News and Courier,* August 31, 1892.

[16] Columbia *Daily Register,* August 7, 1892.

be injured if one of his name already held a seat in that body.

The general election of 1892 offers little of special interest. True to their promise of the previous spring, the anti-Tillmanites put no independent ticket in the field. Although Tillmanism had been defined as "the unholy alliance of a minority of the Democratic party with the solid third party vote of the State," and although Tillman at the national Democratic convention of the previous summer had opposed Cleveland, the successful candidate for the presidential nomination, the Tillmanites loyally supported Cleveland. The Populists, with James B. Weaver as their candidate, received only a thirtieth of the vote of the state.[17]

Governor Tillman, in his first message to the new legislature, forgetting the passions of the previous summer, contented himself with the statement of concrete reforms he wished achieved. His first words were concerned with the facts of revenue adjustment. He expressed his opposition to the tendency of the courts to interfere, by issuing mandamuses in the interest of certain banks which had complained of overassessments, with his attempt to assess all property at its true value. The proper procedure, he believed, was for the banks to be forced to appeal to juries. "While

[17] *Reports and Resolutions,* 1892, II. 343.

we are powerless to apply this remedy to those under the jurisdiction of Federal courts," he said, "we can apply this remedy to their counterpart in South Carolina." He believed that another cause of his failure to arrive at more equitable assessments was the success of some in dodging taxes. This evil could be remedied, he believed, if the government of the counties should be intrusted to boards of township commissioners or selectmen whose first duty should be a reassessment of property at its actual value.

Concerning South Carolina College, he spoke with prophetic good sense. The hope of the trustees, he said, that there would be an increase in the number of applicants for admission into that institution had not been gratified, for the number of students had declined to seventy. The causes of this decline were the great financial stringency under which the state suffered, the fact that the majority cherished prejudices against an institution located in the capital city, the fact that many who had hitherto sent their sons to the institution declined to do so because of its reorganization in 1890, and the preference of many for denominational colleges. The Governor believed that the degree of prosperity which the institution would achieve depended upon the degree to which it might overcome these handicaps, a prediction which its subsequent history has justified.[18]

[18] *House Journal*, 1892, pp. 13-20.

This message was recognized as conservative in tone and vigorous in style. "It was well written," said the *State*.[19] "He [Tillman] has gifts of expression which enable him to declare himself honestly and heartily."

That the new legislature was not to manifest any of the stubborn characteristics of the previous body was proven by the facility with which the Governor secured the two-thirds of both bodies necessary to authorize a popular referendum to determine whether a constitutional convention should be held.[20] The efforts of the conservatives to insert a provision that the proposed constitution be submitted to the people for ratification was voted down.[21]

The administration's railroad regulation bill, introduced as a substitute for the frustrated measure of the previous session, met with furious opposition from the conservatives. The new project provided for a railroad commission of three to be elected by the legislature for their first term and afterwards by the people. The commission was to be given power to examine all schedules and books of the railroad companies in order to fix fair freight and passenger rates and prevent unjust discriminations in charges.[22] The *News*

[19] Columbia *State*, December 4, 1892.
[20] *Acts and Joint Resolutions*, 1892, p. 201.
[21] Columbia *Daily Register*, December 9, 1892.
[22] *Acts and Joint Resolutions*, 1892, pp. 8-17.

and Courier said, "The monstrous injustice of this bill toward the largest and most important interest of the State will drive out capital."[23] A railroad official said,[24] "It puts property rights and interests at the mercy of three men who can ruin us and wipe out values of millions of dollars of property from a whim of their own, or in obedience to a temporary gust of public wrath." The railroad workers protested against a measure that they believed would injure their positions. But Tillman and the legislature remained obdurate. "The opposition of 8,000 or 10,000 railroad employees," said Tillman,[25] "does not amount to a damn compared with 50,000 or 60,000 farmers demanding the passage of this bill." The bill passed. The predictions of the alarmists did not come true, as conservative men were made members of the commission, and no capital was driven from the state. South Carolina was merely given a railroad law like those already enacted in western states.

The Governor's recommendations concerning fiscal reform found expression in an act providing for the forfeiture of the charters of corporations which refused to pay taxes assessed by the state authorities. This involved him in a lengthy controversy with the railroad companies and the

[23] *News and Courier,* December 8, 1892.
[24] *Ibid.,* December 13, 1892.
[25] Columbia *State,* December 15, 1892.

courts. The companies, asserting that the assessments were unjust, paid what they considered just and retired behind the protection of the Federal courts. The Governor then authorized his sheriffs to levy upon the corporations in defiance of the courts. "The unholy alliance," he said, "which exists between the dignity of Federal courts and these harlot corporations must be annulled." But when the sheriffs attempted to act, they were adjudged in contempt of court and fined. With the weight of the courts against him, the Governor acknowledged defeat by paying the fines of the sheriffs.[26]

Against the opposition of the conservative classes, the Tillman legislature made a beginning in the direction of social legislation by passing a bill limiting the hours of labor in the cotton mills. This bill, introduced by "Citizen Josh" Ashley, a sagacious individual who could neither read nor write,[27] was an indication of the growing political importance of the increasing number of poor whites then being concentrated in mill villages. Tillman, although never having shown much interest in the welfare of what he called "the damn

[26] *House Journal*, 1894, p. 9.

[27] Ashley was a typical representative of the rising white democracy of the up-country. Although illiterate and clownish, he was practical, intelligent, and a man of considerable wealth. A radical champion of the poor whites, he was notorious for his alleged holding of Negroes in peonage, and in 1912 he became known for having led a lynching party without the interference of Blease, then governor.

factory class," was willing to champion legislation that met the opposition of mill executives of the type of Orr. The original bill, which provided for the limitation of labor to sixty hours per week, was described by the *News and Courier*[28] "as a bill to discourage manufacturing." "A ten hour law," declared a cotton mill president, "would ruin every mill in the State." But the mill president got a vehement answer to his prediction from Cole L. Blease, who said, "If we have to buy capital by murdering women and children, for God's sake let it go, let it go!" The bill, after a compromise in which the maximum of hours of labor per week was extended to sixty-six, passed.[29]

Perhaps the bill of the two sessions of this legislature which created most ill feeling was a measure proposing that the existing system of congressional districts, by which Charleston was placed in a district with counties of greater white population, be abolished in favor of a system which would place Charleston in a district composed of neighboring counties with huge black majorities. This was interpreted by conservatives "as a plan of devilish ingenuity designed to give Charleston a black congressman." In deference to the protests of the proud city, the bill was abandoned at the 1892 session.[30] But it was re-

[28] November 25, 1892.

[29] *Acts and Joint Resolutions,* 1893, pp. 345-46.

[30] *News and Courier,* December 6, 1892.

vived at the following session in a modified form, and Charleston was placed in a district with a 68,000 black majority.[31] Yet the prediction that a black congressman would again represent the city did not become true.

However indignant the members may have felt toward a governor who treated them with no more courtesy than he had treated their predecessors, they were too prudent to manifest openly insurgent tendencies, for they had reasons to fear that they might be punished as the "driftwood" legislature had been. The county governments were reorganized on a basis akin to that recommended.[32] The state debt of $5,500,000 was refunded at four and one-half per cent. in spite of the attempt of South Carolina bankers to discredit the new régime in Wall Street.[33] Although the pensions of the Confederate veterans were increased and a storm-stricken section of the coast exempted from taxation, the tax levy was decreased by one half a mill.[34] Salaries of public officials were cut ten per cent.[35]

The zeal which Tillman had manifested during his first administration against lynching underwent a revision during his second; or, rather, he

[31] *Acts and Joint Resolutions,* 1893, p. 414.
[32] *Ibid.,* 1893, pp. 481-91.
[33] *Reports and Resolutions,* 1893. II. 664.
[34] *Acts and Joint Resolutions,* 1894, p. 777.
[35] *Ibid.,* 1894, p. 773.

returned to ideas he had cherished during Reconstruction. During the canvass of 1892, he had said, "There is only one crime which warrants lynching, and Governor as I am, I would lead a mob to lynch the negro who ravishes a white woman."[36] When the first lynching of this administration did occur, that of John Peterson, at Denmark, Barnwell County, who was charged with rape, the Governor's conduct seemed to indicate that these words had been more than a bait to the Negro-hating sections of the people. Peterson, after asking for and receiving the Governor's protection, was imprudently turned over to the Barnwell County authorities, from whom he was taken and lynched. The Columbia *State* and a mass meeting of Columbia citizens accused the Governor of connivance with the mob.[37] Tillman expressed himself as of the opinion that the making of an investigation of the affair would serve no useful purpose in view of the state of the public mind,[38] a statement no doubt true. The investigation which he did authorize came to naught, just as hundreds of investigations of a like nature made before and since in the South have come to naught.

That Tillman's words about lynching and his attitude in this case were reprehensible, there can

[36] At Aiken, *News and Courier,* July 7, 1892.
[37] Columbia *State,* April 26, 1893.
[38] *News and Courier,* April 27, 1893.

be no doubt. The difference between the record of no lynchings during his first administration and sixteen lynchings[39] during his second administration may be explained in part by his change of attitude. Yet there is some logic in his position, taken in connection with the view widely held in the South of proper inter-racial relations. This view, cherished by both Tillman and his enemies, was that black blood should not be mixed with that of the pure and superior race. A summary and vivid vengeance, reasoned Tillman, must be executed on the black man who made such an attempt. He had contempt for those Southerners who denounced lynching in the name of law, as he believed that "those who so loudly denounce the course of the Denmark lynchers would be the very first to demand speedy vengeance were some fiend to ravish one who was dear to them."[40]

The campaign of 1894 gave Tillman opportunity to seek popular ratification of the acts of his second administration. He was able to defeat M. C. Butler for the seat which the latter held in the United States Senate as decisively as he had defeated Sheppard in 1892.[41] He took full advantage of the wave of Populistic and anti-Cleve-

[39] *Thirty Years of Lynching in the United States,* p. 88, gives partial figures which have been supplemented by researches in the *News and Courier,* 1892-93.

[40] Columbia *Daily Register,* April 28, 1893.

[41] The vote in the General Assembly was Tillman 131, Butler 21. *House Journal,* 1894, p. 151.

land sentiment, which at that time moved the Democratic masses,[42] and of the characteristic Tillman trick of provoking his adversary to angry outbursts in order that he (Tillman) might come back with effective denunciations. So discouraged were the anti-Tillmanites that in many counties they put no legislative candidates in the field, although Butler's election was contingent upon the control of the legislature.[43] Likewise, they put up no candidate in the contest for governor. The contest for this office was among four Tillman partisans—William H. Ellerbe, John Gary Evans, J. E. Tindal, and Sampson Pope. It resolved itself into a battle as to who could win the support of Tillman and the consequent approval of the voters. In order to accomplish this purpose, the candidates vied with each other in favoring those doctrines of the Farmers' Alliance, which Tillman accepted, and in rejecting those which he rejected, in championing the measures of his administration, and in imitating his manners and his style of public speech.

Tillman, embarrassed, assumed an attitude of neutrality, saying: "They ought to be spanked

[42] "I haven't got words", said Tillman at Rock Hill, June 18, "to say what I think of that old bag of beef [President Cleveland]. If you send me to the Senate, I promise I won't be bulldozed [by him]." Augusta *Chronicle,* June 18, 1894.

[43] The debates between Butler and Tillman appear in the Augusta *Chronicle, News and Courier,* and Columbia *Daily Register,* June 18 to August 15, 1894.

for quarrelling about who is the closest friend of Tillman."[44] However, privately he felt it his duty to support Ellerbe, because, he said, "I was put into office by the Farmers' Movement and my successor ought to be a farmer."[45] But this candidate proved himself "a bashful backwoodsman, halting and inexperienced in speech," while Evans, his chief rival, developed qualities which attracted Tillman to him. He was a nephew of Martin Gary, and, as a member of both houses of the General Assembly, had served Tillman faithfully and capably. He was able to stir his audiences by the keenness of his apprehensions and the brightness of his remarks and, at the same time, was as willing as any candidate to give Tillman the necessary assurance that he as governor would act as his chief bade him. In addition, he was able to win to his side the artful Irby, who pulled for him the necessary wires of the Tillman machine. The result was that Tillman's influence was thrown to him, and such popular feeling as developed against making a lawyer the heir of an agricultural movement was checkmated by the refusal of Tillman to comply with the request of the other candidates that the nomination be made by primary and by his promise to make Ellerbe Evans' successor. Evans was nominated without

[44] Augusta *Chronicle,* July 25, 1894.

[45] Testimony of George R. Koester in *Greenville Piedmont,* September 26, 1916.

JOHN GARY EVANS

opposition by the Democratic convention of September[46] and was elected in October over Pope, who ran as an independent candidate, by an overwhelming majority.[47] Well might Tillman, in the light of such events, declare before the nation: "I represent the State, and I represent it so thoroughly that I claim to give it voice."[48]

Tillman, November 27, 1894, when he turned over the governorship to Evans, took occasion, in his final message to the General Assembly, to give an estimate of his achievements as governor of South Carolina for four years. Aside from those of the first two years, already summarized,[49] he had in his second two years well nigh completed the reforms he had set out to achieve. The railroad regulation bill had been enacted; public expenditures had been reduced; the county administrations had been reorganized, the congressional districts redrawn, a labor law adopted, and a successor after his own heart elected. The passing of the resolution for calling the constitutional convention had paved the way for additional reforms and for enactment into more permanent form of the reforms already achieved.[50] In addition, the unique solution which he had proposed

[46] *News and Courier,* September 2, 1894.

[47] The vote was Evans 39,507, Pope 17,278. *Reports and Resolutions,* 1894, I. 149.

[48] *Congressional Record,* XXXIII. 4659.

[49] See the last paragraph of chapter vi.

[50] See chapter ix,

for the liquor problem had been put into operation.[51] Although the road which he had traveled as governor had been as hard, perhaps, as that of any governor since or before Chamberlain,[52] he had been as much to blame for his difficulties as any of those who met him with "scowling faces," for he had gone to no pains to modify his harsh rural manners in deference to the conventions of the capital city. Nevertheless, his administrations had been a great success, because of his redeeming qualities of good sense, hard work, rigid honesty, and tenacious boldness. Truly it was most proper for him to appeal, as he said, to the "just historian of the future to sustain my good name and to give credit for the good things I have accomplished.[53]

[51] See chapter viii.

[52] "I meet scowling faces when I walk on Main Street", he said to a friend in 1892 in speaking of the manner in which the people of Columbia received him.

[53] *House Journal,* 1894, pp. 12-18, contains his last message to the General Assembly.

CHAPTER VIII

THE DISPENSARY

The most unusual achievement of Tillman's two terms as governor of South Carolina was the inauguration in 1893 of the State Dispensary System through which the state of South Carolina undertook a monopoly of the sale of alcoholic liquors.

This system was instituted in the face of a gradually achieved conviction on the part of a majority of the people in favor of the absolute prohibition of the liquor traffic. Efforts towards the elimination of this traffic may be said to have begun in 1740 with an act prohibiting the sale of intoxicants to slaves except on the authorization of their masters.[1] This was followed, in 1801, by the imposition of a special license tax on spirits.[2] The growth of Prohibition sentiment in the decade before the Civil War is evidenced by the agitations of so prominent a jurist as Belton O'Neall and of other prominent leaders in the evangelical churches. In 1854 Prohibition was

[1] *Acts and Joint Resolutions,* 1740, No. 670.

[2] *Ibid.,* 1801, No. 1762.

effected in a section of Abbeville District.[3] The sale of intoxicants in rural districts was prohibited in 1880; an act in 1882 provided an easy method through which communities might establish Prohibition;[4] this system was temporarily adopted by Barnwell and Oconee Counties in 1883, and had been permanently adopted by Marlboro and Williamsburg Counties and by seventy-six lesser communities by 1891.[5] In that year the Prohibitionists were strong enough to force through the House of Representatives a bill providing for state-wide Prohibition, but this proposal was rejected by the more conservative Senate. The next achievement of these reformers was the inducement of the state Democratic authorities to place a separate box at each polling place of the primary election of 1892, so that the people might express their opinion on the question of state-wide Prohibition. A great majority voted in favor of the proposal.[6]

Armed with this popular mandate and with a clear majority in both houses of the legislature, the Prohibitionists introduced, early in 1892, a most stringent Prohibition bill. In spite of the

[3] The town of Due West, *Ibid.*, 1854, No. 30.

[4] *Ibid.*, 1881-1882, pp. 893-895; 1880, No. 374.

[5] *Ibid., passim*, 1883-1891.

[6] By vote of 38,988 to 29,527, although only a total of 68,515 out of 88,474 who voted in the primary troubled themselves to vote on the question of Prohibition. Columbia *State*, September 10, 1892.

opposition of the experienced members from the cities, the bill, after a lengthy discussion, passed the House. For eight days, until three days before adjournment, the Senate struggled over it. Then, without any previous indication of his intent, John Gary Evans informed the two houses that Governor Tillman desired the passage of an unknown Dispensary law as a substitute for the Prohibition bill.[7]

The manner in which Tillman became convinced of the wisdom of an act so at variance with the traditional individualism of South Carolina is most interesting. In 1865, and afterwards, certain Swedish cities adopted the Gothenburg system of municipal monopoly of the sale of liquors. In 1885, in order to meet the special problems of a college town, Athens, Georgia, had adopted with success a modified form of this system. Tillman, although in principle a well-known opponent of Prohibition, had, previous to the opening of the legislature of 1892, tactfully avoided taking any part in the liquor controversy. Through the influence of Larry Gantt, who had lived in Athens, Tillman became convinced of the benefits of the Athens plan. It would, Gantt said,[8] substantially increase the revenue of the state and thereby afford Tillman an easy means of keeping his

[7] *News and Courier* and Columbia *State,* December 22-25, 1892.
[8] Columbia *Daily Register,* November 30, 1892.

pledge to reduce the taxes; by decreasing the consumption of strong drink, it would be a wise compromise between the Prohibition and saloon factions. Accordingly, in his first message to the legislature of 1892, Tillman advocated the system in general terms.[9]

The manner in which the law was passed is an interesting commentary on the Governor's ability to enforce obedience to his will. He was opposed by a majority of the people and of the legislature —which included both the advocates of Prohibition and of the saloons. In addition, the legislature had already decided to enact Prohibition and was unable to understand this very strange piece of new legislation in the short time given for its consideration; furthermore, it was not desirous of doing the will of the high-handed Governor, for whom the body had no personal love. But Tillman was able to effect his wish because of his hold upon the popular imagination and because a majority of the legislature, who owed their positions to him, feared that he might order their defeat in the next election. Operating from his office in "the lower regions of the State House," he, through personal admonitions administered individually in the strongest of language, forced the more recalcitrant of his partisans to support the bill. The result was that, when the legislature

[9] *House Journal,* 1892, p. 15.

adjourned on Christmas Eve, the Dispensary system was a part of the law of South Carolina.[10]

The Dispensary act[11] gave to the state the monopoly of the liquor traffic. A state board of control, composed of the governor and two other state officials, was given supervision of the institution, and a Dispensary commissioner was placed in active control. In each county in which one or more dispensaries were to be established, a county board of control was created with authority to appoint the dispensers and their assistants. To be eligible for the position of dispenser, one had to prove that he did not drink and was not liable by present or past connections to be privately interested in the liquor business. A majority of the electors of any township could prevent the establishment of a dispensary in their midst. In a county which had previously prohibited the liquor traffic, a petition of one-fourth of the citizens and a vote of a majority of the electors could effect the establishment of a branch of the institution. A person desiring to purchase liquor was to be required to file an application with the dispenser, stating the quantity and kind of liquor wanted. If the applicant was intoxicated or given to using liquor in excess, he was to be granted no sale. The liquor had to be sold in sealed packages not

[10] *News and Courier,* and Columbia *State,* December 21-26, 1892, contain full accounts of the manner in which this law was enacted.

[11] *Acts and Joint Resolutions,* 1892, pp. 61-67; 1893, pp. 430-450.

to be opened on the premises. Constables appointed by the governor, in such numbers as he deemed sufficient, were charged with the prevention of private sales. If the state board of control deemed a municipality negligent in the enforcement of the prohibition against private sales, it could withdraw the municipality's share of the Dispensary revenue. The profits of retail sales were to be evenly divided between counties and municipalities, and those accruing from the state's handling of the liquors were to go to the state treasury. The act was to go into effect July 1, 1893.

The Governor, in his effort to put into operation such an unprecedented act of state socialism, met with the most determined opposition. The individualistic people of South Carolina had overnight been served notice that they must drink under regulation and give into the public treasury profits which had previously gone to private individuals. The Columbia *State* immediately began its fourteen-year task of doing the Dispensary to death. The *News and Courier*[12] predicted that such an act of legislation would never go into effect; while the municipal authorities of Charleston and several other towns issued licenses for saloons to operate six months after the date on which the law required that they be closed. A convention of

[12] January 24, 1893.

nine hundred bar owners pledged themselves to do all in their power to defeat the law;[13] while the most influential of the Prohibition organs[14] called it "a just cause for lamentation," and a Baptist congregation expelled from its membership the man whom Tillman had appointed Dispensary commissioner.[15] The difficulties of the Governor were increased by the fact that the inhabitants of the towns had always been hostile to him and anything he advocated, and it was in towns only that the law permitted dispensaries to be established.

But Tillman boldly went about the task of putting the law into operation. "The barrooms of the State," he said, "will be closed after July 1, and the law will be enforced to the limit." He appointed a thorough business man, who was the husband of a prominent official of the Woman's Christian Temperance Union, as Dispensary commissioner. Desiring to use to the best advantage the meager $50,000 which the legislature had appropriated for the purchase of the initial stock of liquors, he journeyed to Louisville and Cincinnati to supervise personally the purchases. Although himself a teetotaler, he demonstrated sufficient knowledge of the grades of liquors to accomplish his task. "If I catch you monkeying with your agreements," he rudely told a distiller

[13] *News and Courier,* January 8, 1893.
[14] *Baptist Courier,* January 4, 1893.
[15] *News and Courier,* October 24, 1893.

who had extended him credit, "I will quit you and won't buy a gallon." Under his personal supervision a building was equipped for bottling the liquors as they were received.[16] In those municipalities in which the law permitted the operation of dispensaries, buildings were provided with the necessary fittings. "There can be no doubt," admitted the *News and Courier*[17] "that everything about the Dispensary is done in the most improved and business-like manner." As the date for the opening approached, Tillman gathered the badges and arms necessary for the use of the constables whom he might find it necessary to dispatch to any place in which the law did not work smoothly. "I will make the places that won't accept the Dispensary," he said,[18] "dry enough to burn. I will send special constables if I have to cover every city block with a separate man." The result was that the dispensaries opened on schedule.

But trouble soon grew out of the activities of the constables. The newspapers incited the people, always tenacious of their traditions of individual liberty, to resist searches of their dwellings. "The spies," as the constables were called,

[16] From Tillman's testimony before a legislative committee appointed in 1906 to investigate the Dispensary. *Reports and Resolutions,* 1906, III. 304-312.

[17] July 16, 1893.

[18] New York *Sun,* July 9, 1893.

were pictured as "monsters," and casualties, incurred in their efforts to enforce the law, were "murders." "Our bloody Governor" was portrayed as presiding over stores of ammunition to be used against the defenders of the public liberties.[19] "The people," said the Columbia *State,* "will know that if the Governor's armed spies enter their homes, insult their women and shoot down their sons or brothers, they will be promptly pardoned."[20] "I'll be —," said even the brother of the Governor, "if I don't shoot the first spy who enters my residence and opens my package of goods."[21] Insurrection was brewing.

And it came in less than a year after the law went into effect. As the result of the resentment growing out of the execution of search warrants in the town of Darlington, a riot occurred between the constables and a mob of citizens, March 30, 1894. In the interchange of shots two citizens and a constable were killed and several citizens wounded. When the constables fled before the mob, the enraged citizens, aided by other enemies of the Dispensary who had been summoned by bells and telegrams, began a man hunt.

At five o'clock on the same day the Governor and the people of Columbia received the news. Tillman, faced with the duty of preventing the

[19] Columbia *State,* January 1, 1894.
[20] January 28, 1894.
[21] *News and Courier,* January 16, 1894.

possible lynching of the agents of the law, acted promptly. He ordered the three militia companies of the city to move to Darlington by special train. Meantime the people of the city, already hostile to the Governor and to the Dispensary, had been stirred to fury by the inflammatory bulletins of the *State*. The companies, intimidated by threats of the populace and acting on the advice of such an important citizen as Bishop Capers, refused to obey the call. This was followed by the news that the militia of the other towns, who had been ordered to board the special train, likewise had refused to obey. The General of the Charleston militia telegraphed the Governor, "My command will not lend itself to foster civil war among our brethren."

Failing in his efforts to exact obedience from the organized militia, the Governor ordered the mobilization of men of the rural districts from which he drew his political strength. In spite of the threats of angry crowds who swore that no companies should go to Darlington, he was able, by the morning of the second day, to concentrate 475 of his "wool hat" militia in the state prison and to place a guard of the Edgefield Hussars, his old command, to protect the Governor's Mansion against the mob. These events were followed by the threat of a mob led by J. C. Haskell to storm the prison, and the declaration by the Governor that the counties of Darlington and Florence were "in open rebellion." Three days after the disobedience of the regular militia, a regiment of improvised militia moved to Darlington, only to find their presence unnecessary, as the town had become quiet and the constables had escaped without injury.

The Governor dealt firmly with the disobedient militia. The officers were dismissed, the rank and file disarmed, and in their place a hundred rural companies were organized. The "costly farce" of a court martial was not attempted, as the punishment of so large and so influential an element of the state's population was obviously impossible.[22]

The "Dispensary War" threw into sharp relief the bitter antagonisms which divided the people of South Carolina. Conservative men had attempted to lynch the agents of their government, and the militia had mutinied. The Governor showed himself determined to enforce the hated law to the extent of violating individual liberties and supporting constables who fired into crowds. Yet he had won a victory for the supremacy of law and the enforcement of the Dispensary system. He lost none of his popularity among the rural masses of the state, and the press of the outside world, hitherto hostile to him, applauded his

[22] For these events we have used the Columbia *Daily Register*, *State*, and the *News and Courier*, March 30 to April 15, 1894; Tillman MS., "The Darlington Riot"; "Message of 1894," *Senate Journal*, 1894, pp. 18-40.

firm stand. Said the London *Spectator:*[23] "The rebellion seems to be over, thanks to the prompt action of Governor Tillman. . . . He has grit."

No less troublesome than the popular hostility to Tillman's law was the hostility of the courts. At the time of the Darlington riot a circuit judge had already enjoined the county board of control for Darlington County from operating a dispensary, basing his action on the belief that a state monopoly for trade was unconstitutional. However, the newly-elected Tillman member of the state Supreme Court suspended the injunction, pending a decision from the full court. Less than three weeks after the Darlington riot—at a time when the Dispensary was in greatest disrepute—the Supreme Court, by a vote of two anti-Tillman partisans to one Tillman partisan, declared the law unconstitutional.[24] Tillman was forced to obey. Four days after the decision, he ordered the dispensaries closed. As the court had only declared those portions of the law unconstitutional which permitted the state to engage in the liquor traffic, the sections prohibiting private sales remained in force. The state now enjoyed legal Prohibition, although no attempt was made to enforce it.[25]

[23] May 16, 1894.

[24] *McCullough* vs. *Brown,* 41, S. C., 220.

[25] As proved by the fact that the national government, between April 21 and August 1, 1894, issued 1174 liquor licenses for South Carolina.

But Tillman had anticipated the action of the court. He had used his influence with the legislature of 1893 to effect the defeat of Justice McGowan and the election in his place of Eugene B. Gary and the passage of a new Dispensary Act to replace the one which the court had under review. This did not prevent the adverse decision of the court, as McGowan's term of office did not expire until the first of the following August, but it did make certain that after that date the new law could be put in force and that a decision favorable to it could be exacted from a court two to one in Tillman's favor. Accordingly, on August 1, 1894, the Dispensary act of 1893 was declared in force. This was followed by a decision, written by Justice Gary, declaring that the Dispensary was constitutional, because a public monopoly was a legitimate part of the police power of a state.[26] Tillman, in explaining his conduct, frankly admitted that "the same general principle underlay both acts, and that if one was unconstitutional the other was also. . . . [But] a change in the Courts made me feel it my duty to revise the Act of 1892."[27]

Tillman was able to leave office in 1894 with the Dispensary triumphant over the wrath of the people and the courts.[28]

[26] *State* vs. *Aiken,* 42, S. C., 222.

[27] *Senate Journal,* 1894, pp. 31. 33.

[28] In 1897 the United States Supreme Court declared the law constitutional. *Vance* vs. *Vandercock,* 170, U. S., 438.

During the fourteen years of existence of the Dispensary the average annual profit derived by the state from the liquor business was $465,600, which was double the amount which the state in 1892 had derived from the sale of liquor licenses.[29] The distribution of liquor revenues was more even than had been the case previously, and the state government for the first time received a share. A government pledged to the reduction of taxation was able to meet more adequately the demands of the progressive South, especially the demands for education, since a portion of the liquor revenue, after 1900, was used for this purpose.

Although there was a substantial increase in revenue, there can be no doubt that it would have been greater had not corruption and inefficiency crept into the administration. The Dispensary was born in a welter of politics, and it was but natural that the successors of the man who had emphasized the importance of political partisanship as a means of selecting the managers of a great public business should be inefficient, or even dishonest politicians. In addition, South Carolina lacked the expert bureaucracy which has enabled many European communities to operate successfully such ventures in state socialism. Consequently, when the South Carolina politician was

[29] The profits from the saloons for the fiscal year ending December 31, 1892 were $215,472. *Reports and Resolutions, passim,* 1892-1907.

given an opportunity to participate in business on a large scale, many irregularities occurred. In 1906, a legislative committee discovered that rebates had been paid by agents of wholesale liquor houses to agents of the Dispensary. "It required something more than good liquor to get the business," said a whiskey merchant.[30] Irresponsible clerks bought more whiskey than was necessary.[31] When the accounts of the Dispensary were settled in 1910, many distillers were forced to pay fines to the state in compensation for irregularities. These and numerous other instances of corruption and inefficiency led a commission of the legislature to declare that the officials of the Dispensary "have become shameless in their abuse of power, insatiable in their greed and perfidious in the discharge of their oath of office."[32]

The establishment of the Dispensary tended to decrease the consumption of strong drink—to what degree we cannot be certain. The attractions of the barrooms were abolished; for them were substituted the unadorned dispensaries, in which no loafing was allowed and from which liquors were sold only in sealed packages, ostensibly only to persons who did not use alcohol to excess. In 1892 there were 613 bars in the state; there were never more than 146 dispensaries. In

[30] *Reports and Resolutions*, 1906, III. 296.
[31] *Ibid.*, 1910, III. 280.
[32] *Ibid.*, 1910, III. 282.

a two months period of the first year in which the Dispensary was in operation the number of arrests for drunkenness, in eighteen towns, fell from 576, the record of the previous year, to 283.[33] These figures should be taken as indicating that the Dispensary under the vigorous administration of Tillman decreased the excessive consumption of liquors.

That the law continued to hold in check the consumption of spirits is very doubtful. The regulations as to whom liquors might be sold were not enforced. In spite of the continued activity of the constables, "blind tigers" and "clubs" for the sale of liquors flourished in the towns with the support of local opinion. A foreign observer reported the general standard of enforcement as low and told of "saloon keepers who call themselves druggists and sell liquors to all comers for medical purposes."[34]

The fact that South Carolina abolished the state Dispensary in 1907,[35] and its substitute, the county dispensaries, in 1915, in favor of statewide Prohibition[36] is, however, no proof that the Dispensary was *per se* a failure. In spite of lax

[33] Tillman, "The South Carolina Liquor Law", *North American Review,* CLVIII. 145 (February, 1894).

[34] E. L. Fanshowe, *Liquor Legislation in the United States,* pp. 356-57.

[35] *Acts and Joint Resolutions,* 1907, pp. 463-81.

[36] *Ibid.,* 1915, pp. 88-90; *Reports and Resolutions,* 1916, II. 715-16.

management, it was always profitable, and surely capable officials could have been found to handle its yearly expenditures of $2,500,000. The real reason for its abolition was the continued growth of the Prohibition sentiment among the white masses, a sentiment which would have asserted itself had there been no Dispensary. Tillman, in 1892, at the height of his power, had overridden this sentiment, and at every election after that year until 1906 was able to elect candidates for governor pledged to the retention of the Dispensary. He appealed to the tendency of many to regard drinking as a necessity and Prohibition as an undue restriction on personal liberty, made use of the political machine behind him, wrote vigorous letters to the people, and testified before a legislative committee in behalf of the system.[37] Nevertheless, Prohibition triumphed. The increased education which the people had received inculcated a greater respect for public order and morality. Such societies as the Woman's Christian Temperance Union advocated the wisdom of total abstinence, and the Methodist and Baptist clergy taught the moral value of Prohibition. The fact that Tillman had taught the plain people how to exercise their political power made possible a more speedy enactment into law of their will con-

[37] Testimony in *Reports and Resolutions,* 1906, III; letter in the Columbia *State,* August 10, 1904.

cerning his cherished institution than would have been the case had there been no Tillman to upset the political arrangement of the eighties, which had given political power to a group less inclined toward Prohibition.

CHAPTER IX

THE CONSTITUTIONAL CONVENTION

The constitution of 1868, although it was made by a convention the majority of which was colored, remained as the fundamental law of South Carolina for nineteen years after 1877, the year the whites recovered complete control of the government. Why this constitution, like so many other relics of Negro rule, was not sooner abolished needs explanation. First, from a theoretical viewpoint it was an excellent document, being based on the constitution of a liberal northern commonwealth, Ohio. Second, such innovations as representation according to population and universal free education, which it introduced, were satisfactory to most whites after Reconstruction. Again, conservative South Carolinians had gradually adopted as their own many of the liberal principles which this constitution imposed upon them. Moreover, they feared that they might incur punishments like those of Reconstruction in case they were too hasty in undoing such a major achievement of the Republicans. Finally, after 1886, they refused to give the two-thirds vote of both houses of the legislature necessary for a change, because they preferred the old constitution to any which might be made by the Tillmanites.

After the complete triumph of Tillmanism, the making of a new constitution was inevitable. The white democracy insisted upon even greater restrictions, social and political, upon the Negro than the conservatives had effected. After 1885, the most reiterated demand of Tillman was that this sentiment be expressed in a fundamental law —a law to be made by white hands only, which should give constitutional recognition to restrictions on Negro suffrage and social equality. The triumph of this demand, however, did not come until 1893, when, as we have already said, the resolution for a popular vote as to whether a constitutional convention should be held became law.

The battle between opponents and proponents of a constitutional convention was a main issue in the campaign of 1894. Although in that year Tillman won with ease a seat in the United States Senate, the fight over the convention question was hard and close. The anti-Tillmanites fought valiantly to preserve the state from the permanent influence of Tillman; the Negroes fought to preserve their last political hopes. Larry Gantt, although still a friend of Tillman and even more radical than he in his opposition to the Negro in politics, opposed the convention on the grounds that it was impossible to impose a restriction upon Negro suffrage which would stand the test of the United States Supreme Court and at the same time allow the poor white man to vote. "When you take away the ballots of the poor man," said this champion of white democracy,[1] "you strip him of his armor and place him at the mercy of the money power." But Tillman had counter arguments. He deplored the day when "white men of acknowledged character and decent reputation are willing to use the Negro in politics with the hope of regaining lost supremacy." Such a tendency already had been manifested in the Haskell movement of 1890 and the Pope movement of 1894. "The black ghosts of Reconstruction," he said in urging the necessity of the disfranchisement of the Negro, "would run forth and devour white civilization as soon as the impending white disunity became an inevitable fact."[2] He won his fight for the convention by a vote of 31,402 to 29,523.[3]

Tillman's next task was to make certain that a majority of the delegates to the convention should be in favor of his plans to eliminate the Negro from politics, and, second, that they should be willing to act as his own partisans. In order to

[1] Columbia *Daily Register,* September 6, 1894.

[2] *News and Courier,* October 7, 1894.

[3] *Reports and Resolutions,* 1894, II. 472.

accomplish this double purpose, he appealed to the anti-Tillmanites. He was a wise enough statesman to know that probably the best legal intelligence of the state was found among the conservatives and that a constitution made with a minimum amount of partisanship was more likely to have permanent value than if, like the Dispensary, it were made in a welter of partisanship. Likewise, he feared that the conservatives, in case they were not treated fairly, would appeal to the Negro in the general election. In addition to these manifestations of "farseeing statesmanship," Tillman, in calling the conservatives to his side, was looking after his own political interests. At that stage of his career, there were as many Tillmanites who secretly disliked him as there had been among the legislators in 1892. Realizing that they were planning to frustrate him through an appeal to the opposition, Tillman planned to checkmate them by a like appeal.[4] As the first move in this internal struggle, a conference of forty Tillmanite members of the legislature, who were secretly opposed to Tillman, asked that delegates to the constitutional convention, by a mutual understanding in the various counties, be evenly divided between Tillmanites and conservatives.[5]

[4] For this interpretation the author depends on the testimony of Hon. Thomas Kirkland, of Camden, who was a member of the conference of forty legislators.

[5] *News and Courier,* March 28, 1895; Koester, *Greenville Piedmont,* April 14, 1916.

Meanwhile Tillman and Governor Evans met in conference two of their most violent political enemies, Joseph Barnwell and J. C. Hemphill, editor of the *News and Courier,* on February 14, 1895. The four agreed to carry into effect an even division of the representation on condition that the proposed constitution be not submitted to the people and that no provision be inserted in the document which would deprive any portion of the white manhood of suffrage.[6] So great was the prestige of Tillman that this counter-proposal brought about the collapse of the plan of the forty insurgent legislators. The conservative compromisers felt that only through Tillman's influence might they be able to gain additional seats in the convention.

Tillman's plan met with sharp opposition from members of both factions. Gonzales and the supporters of his newspaper refused to accept the agreement, either because they thought that they could defeat Tillman at the polls or because they preferred their own defeat to compromise with one for whom they cherished such extreme personal aversion. The uncompromising Tillmanites found an artful spokesman in Irby, who, in a letter of poignant bitterness, proclaimed his intention not to respect the compromise.[7] Tillman,

[6] *News and Courier,* February 19, 1895.

[7] *Ibid.,* March 12, 1895.

seeing that public opinion was against his move, on March 30, 1895, repudiated his agreement on the grounds that it might lead to the disfranchisement of "illiterate and poor white men" and to "the supremacy of the whole crowd who have been left out in the cold for the past four years."[8] The conservatives charged him with breach of good faith. In view of the fact that later he admitted that the real motive for his repudiation of the agreement was the change in public opinion[9] and that his maneuvers served to discredit the insurgent faction within his party, one can hardly believe that a man of his intense partisan feelings really meant what he said when he agreed to give the opposition half of the delegates.

However, this repudiation of the formal agreement did not prevent Tillman from carrying out his real intention of giving the conservatives some representation. During the canvass for the nomination of Democratic delegates for Edgefield County, Tillman suggested that two of the six nominees be conservatives. This idea was taken up by other pro-Tillman counties, and Richland, the leading conservative county, gave representation to the Tillmanites. Charleston refused. As result of these and other compromises of like nature, the conservatives had forty-three delegates

[8] *News and Courier,* March 30, 1895.

[9] Before the Convention. *Journal of the Constitutional Convention of 1895,* p. 472.

to Tillman's 113. Had the delegates been selected on a basis of strict partisanship, it is very likely that the conservatives would have controlled only the delegations of Richland and Charleston, because Beaufort, one of the two other counties in which they dominated the Democratic party, returned a Negro delegation, and Georgetown, the other, returned two Negroes to two conservatives.

Having made certain the domination by his own faction of the white portion of the coming convention, Tillman next addressed himself to the task of preventing the Negroes from controlling the general election. As we have already said, one of the motives in giving the conservatives representation was to prevent a coalition between dissatisfied whites and the Negroes. An additional precaution against Negro control was the enactment in 1894 of a registration law which provided that persons who had registered since the passage of the Eight Box Law (1882) were to be allowed to vote with little question, which admitted most of the whites; while those who had registered previous to that law, or who had not registered at all, were to be subjected to most baffling rules, which excluded most of the Negroes.[10] The result was that only ten thousand Negroes of the one hundred thousand or more of voting age succeeded in registering.[11] Yet, even

[10] *Acts and Joint Resolutions,* 1894, pp. 804-05.

[11] *News and Courier,* March 15, 1895.

without this law, it is not likely that the Negroes would have been a menace to white domination, as "they had no one to guide them, and neither the courage nor intelligence sufficient to make themselves felt as of any political importance."[12] The evidence of their political activity was small. In January, 1895, a conference of Negro ministers, recognizing the desire of the whites to disfranchise their race, called a convention in protest.[13] As a result of this call, some one hundred black and white Republicans, in convention, denounced the purposes of the whites and called on the Negro "to register to the man."[14] The only effective result of these agitations was the election of a solid Negro delegation from Beaufort and two Negro delegates from Georgetown.

A more serious menace to Tillman's plans was the effort of Sampson Pope to have the election declared illegal. On Pope's motion, Federal Judge Goff declared the election of delegates void on the grounds that the election law of 1894 defeated the constitutional prohibition of the restrictions of suffrage on racial grounds. This decision was followed by "humble rejoicing" on the part of a Negro ministers' union and by Tillman's assertion that the convention would be held, regardless of the decision of "a dirty Republican judge." But

[12] *New York Evening Post,* March 20, 1895.

[13] *News and Courier,* February 7, 1895.

[14] *Ibid.,* May 4-9, 1895.

this latter resolve was unnecessary, as the Federal Circuit Court of Appeals reversed the action of the lower court,[15] and the way was now open for the assembling of the convention.

Accordingly, on September 10, 1895, the third convention of "the people of South Carolina" since the Civil War met to frame a new constitution for the state. The leadership was in the hands of men of much greater experience and ability than was usually found in a legislature. Preëminent among the conservatives were George Tillman and J. C. Sheppard, of Edgefield; George Johnstone, of Newberry; D. S. Henderson, of Aiken; and Theodore Barker and J. K. P. Bryan, of Charleston. Three of the Negro delegates, Thomas Miller, Robert Smalls, and J. W. Whipper, all of Beaufort, occupied prominent places in the convention, because the duty of defending their race against the determination of the whites to effect disfranchisement of the blacks devolved upon them. They upheld their cause with extraordinary ability and conducted themselves with a quiet dignity which the whites rewarded with polite treatment.[16] The real leadership of the convention devolved upon Ben Tillman. A New York observer described him as usually sitting in

[15] *News and Courier,* August 4-8, 1895; *Mills* vs. *Green,* 68 *Federal Reporter,* 818; 69, *Federal Reporter,* 852.

[16] George R. Koester, *Greenville Piedmont,* November 9, 1916, is among the many whites who have praised the conduct of the Negro delegates.

the heart of the assemblage, his feet resting on the top of his desk, and "his one fierce eye watching the six negro delegates whispering in the corner about a new scheme of disfranchisement." He carried his points neither by persuasion nor friendships but by inspiring fear in both friend and foe, whom he lashed with sharp words, and by a wise conservatism destined to provoke neither the hostility of the national courts nor that of white South Carolina.[17] He, as leader of the sovereign body of the state, was as near absolute master of South Carolina as any single individual had ever been, although, as we shall see, he was not always able to carry his point. The other Tillman leaders were Governor Evans, president of the body, Irby, and Jasper Talbert.

The earliest and most important problem before the convention was the writing of a franchise clause satisfactory to Tillman and his followers. This problem was most baffling, in view of the fact that, for the plan to be an improvement over the manner in which the whites already excluded the Negro from voting, it must eliminate the necessity of "fraud and intimidation." Moreover, the elimination of Negroes of all degrees of wealth and intelligence from the suffrage had to be effected without breaking the pledge not to disfranchise the 13,924 illiterate and mostly landless

[17] James Creelman, *New York World,* September 30 and October 6, 1895.

male whites and without coming in conflict with the provision of the Constitution of the United States which prohibited discrimination in suffrage on racial grounds. A simple literacy test would have given the whites control on a basis of law without the necessity of fraud and violence, but it would have excluded some whites and would have admitted many Negroes. The proposal of Robert Aldrich that the Negro be made ineligible to hold office was rejected as obviously unconstitutional. "It would make the Convention," said Tillman, "the laughing stock of the nation."[18] A so-called "grandfather clause," which would give suffrage to those whose ancestors had served in the Confederate or Union armies, or who had voted before the Civil War, was rejected as clumsy. The plan finally adopted was in essential details identical with a provision of the Mississippi constitution of 1890 and was presented by Tillman, chairman of the committee on suffrage, as best fulfilling the requirements of the situation. Every male citizen of South Carolina was given the right to vote provided he came within the following restrictions: He must have lived in the state for two years, the county for one year, have paid his poll tax six months before election, and not have been guilty of such crimes as bigamy,

[18] *Journal of the Constitutional Convention of 1895*, p. 270; *News and Courier*, September 28, 1895. This newspaper published full reports of the debates.

adultery, wife-beating, larceny, and receiving stolen goods. Up to January 1, 1898, a person who fulfilled these qualifications, and who could both read and write any section of the constitution, or could understand it when read by the registration office, was to be a lifetime voter. After that date, the person who had fulfilled the aforementioned qualifications and who could both read and write any section of the constitution to the satisfaction of the registration officer, or could show that he owned and had paid all taxes on property in the state assessed at three hundred dollars or over, could vote.[19] Notwithstanding the efforts of Tillman, who believed such a provision necessary because he believed there would be a split in the ranks of the whites, no provision was made for minority representation on the boards of election. The intent of the general provisions was to exclude many Negroes from the suffrage by disqualifying the voter for crimes of which Negroes frequently were guilty and by providing for rigid residence and poll tax requirements in view of the Negro's habit of frequent change of residence and the tendency of so prodigal a race not to pay taxes so far in advance. The obvious intent of the provision through which a voter could qualify before 1898 was to afford an easy expedient through which the existing mass

[19] *Constitution of 1895,* Art. II.

of landless white illiterates could become voters. The obvious purpose of the permanent provision was, first, to eliminate the Negroes either because they did not pay their poll tax or because they did not own three hundred dollars worth of property, or through the provision which gave white election officials the right to exercise their "discretion" as to whether the applicant could both read and write a section of the constitution, even if in truth he was able to do both. The white man who paid his poll tax but did not own sufficient property or know how to read and write could be allowed to register under the exercise of this "discretion."

Confronted with this flagrant intention to eliminate their race from politics by constitutional enactment, the Negro delegates made a spirited defense of the rights of their people. Thomas Miller defended his race in the name of human justice and equality against those who were "striking at the very roots of universal liberty." "I appeal for justice," he said, "for those whose chief lot has been to toil, toil, toil with no hope but toil." "It was your love of power and your supreme arrogance," he said to the opposition, "which brought it [Reconstruction] upon you. . . . Your hatred has been centered and he [the Negro] is the innocent sufferer of your spleen." W. J. Whipper, an eloquent black man who had been a notorious figure during Reconstruction, was more compromising. He believed the conferring of universal suffrage had been a mistake for which the uncompromising southerner and the doctrinaire Yankee, not the Negro, had been responsible. He commended Tillman for his frankness. Yet he paid tribute to the work of the constitutional convention of 1868, of which he had been a member, and would remind the South that it owed the Negro a debt of gratitude. "It was the brawny arm of the Negro," he said, "which cared for you in your cradle, made your harvest, protected you in your homes, and yet he is the man you propose to rob of his suffrage." Robert Smalls, hero of the Union navy, ex-congressman and another noteworthy figure during Reconstruction, offered compromise. He would have a "fair and honest" election law which would give the whites a majority. But in fairness, he asked that the Tillman scheme be not adopted, for it "would mean that every white man would interpret it right and every Negro wrong."[20]

These speeches were heard by attentive delegates and crowded galleries and given the widest publicity in the newspapers. But they were in vain, for when Smalls moved to modify the Tillman plan, only the other five Negro delegates

[20] Mrs. T. J. Miller, *Speeches of the Negro Delegates.*

voted with him.[21] The whites, pro-Tillman and anti-Tillman, were unanimous in their intent to eliminate the Negro from politics.

November 1, Tillman, impressed with what the Negroes had said, arose to reply. He began with the reminder that the convention had assembled for the purpose of restricting suffrage so as to make it impossible for the "hell-hounds of Reconstruction to re-enact their devilish work." He graphically narrated the oft-repeated story of Reconstruction—"the ring-streaked and striped Carpet-Bagger Convention of 1868," a government officered by "white thieves," the venal incapacity of the black voters, fraudulent bond issues, furniture thefts, etc. Then came terrible thrusts at Smalls and Whipper as illustrations of the venality of Negro rule. The former had taken bribes and had been guilty of "printing steals;" the latter was absolved of one act of corruption only to be accused in detail of the most sordid and grotesque financial irregularities. The Negroes, he continued, could not be acquitted of the wrongs of Reconstruction, for had they not "put the little piece of paper in the box which gave the commission to the white scoundrels who were their leaders?" This connection between white corruptionists and Negro voters "must be our justification, our vindication, our excuse to the world that

[21] *Convention Journal*, p. 420.

we are met in convention openly, boldly and without any pretense of secrecy to announce that it is our purpose so to restrict the suffrage and circumscribe it that this infamy may not come about again."

Less satisfactory than his reply to the Negroes, was his answer to the inquiry of H. C. Patton, a young delegate from Richland, who asked how the Negro illiterates were to be kept from registering and the white illiterates be allowed to do so without "fraud and discrimination," the evils of the old system. Tillman virtually admitted that this evil was not eliminated, saying:

> Some poisons in small doses are very salutary and valuable medicines. . . . The officer [registration officer] is responsible to his conscience and his God; he is responsible to nobody else. . . . It is just showing partiality, perhaps, [laughter] or discrimination. Oh, you grin [turning to Mr. Patton], you of all men to get up here and wrap your Pharisaical robes around you.[22]

The provision as proposed was adopted.[23]

These suffrage restrictions have been successful in all but one respect. The number of Negroes who have since exercised the right of suffrage has been negligible.[24] Negroes no longer sit in the

[22] Tillman's address is published in *Convention Journal,* pp. 443-72; Sheppard's arraignment of the Republican régime, *Ibid.,* pp. 476-80; Smalls' defense of himself, *Ibid.,* pp. 472-76.

[23] *Ibid.,* p. 506.

[24] The Republican vote in 1900 was 3,526; in 1920, 2,244. *World Almanac.* The number of Negroes voting, excluding a few "Hampton negroes," must be less than these figures.

legislature, no longer contesting even the elections of Beaufort County. The election officials did with thoroughness the work that Tillman outlined for them. The constitution proclaims—in words as plain as the constitution of the United States permits—the attitude of white South Carolina toward Negro suffrage. Yet it is hard to believe that it has had a vital effect upon the political status of the Negro. A legal subterfuge together with force kept the blacks from the polls before 1895. Since that date another legal subterfuge and the threat of force have been used.[25] Tillman's prediction that the additional legal safeguards might be necessary, because of a rift in white unity and because of an intransigent black race, have not been substantiated by events.

The next act of the convention was to settle the question of racial intermarriage. When it was suggested that such marriages be prohibited, Smalls suggested that white men guilty of cohabitation with Negro women out of wedlock be disqualified for office-holding and that children born of such unions be given the name of the father. Tillman championed this proposal in a modified form. He said that, although he had "been twitted as the arch-enemy of the negro race," he

[25] That the whites are prepared to use force in keeping the Negroes from the polls is illustrated by the manner in which Negro women were treated in 1920 at Columbia. William Pickens, "The Woman Voter Hits the Color Line," in *The Nation,* CXII. 426-8 (March 23, 1921).

wished "to protect the negro women against the debauchery of white men degrading themselves on a level with black women." But he was voted down, and a simple provision prohibiting miscegenation was passed.[26]

The spirit which prompted Negro disfranchisement found partial expression in the educational provisions of the new document. Separate schools must be provided for the two races; no provision was made for compulsory education; and the local school boards were given power to apportion school funds. This latter provision made possible a steady decline in the proportion of funds given the Negro schools—from two-sevenths in 1899 to slightly over one-tenth in 1920. Yet the generally progressive tendency of the constitution has been of absolute benefit to Negro schools, for the provision of the constitution of 1868 recognizing the obligation of the state to give free education to all was reaffirmed, and it is a fact that almost twice as much was spent for Negro education in 1920 as was spent for all education in 1889.[27]

As a substitute for a proposal to penalize sheriffs from whose hands persons were taken to be lynched, Tillman effected the passage of a pro-

[26] The debate in the *News and Courier,* October 4; November 22, 1895; *Convention Journal,* pp. 618-19.

[27] The facts of this paragraph are gleaned from *Reports of the Superintendent of Education, Reports and Resolutions,* 1889-1920.

vision for the suspension from office of any such sheriffs and for their subsequent removal, if convicted of neglect of duty, and for the penalization, on the judgment of a court, of the county in which a lynching occured, to the extent of not less than $2000, to be distributed to the relatives of the victim.[28] "If we want to stop lynching," said Tillman,[29] "we must prick the consciences of the taxpayers." Although this was the most effective legal remedy that could have been conceived, the number of judgments obtained in consequence of the eighty-odd lynchings which have since occurred in the state have been few. It has been deemed wise to appeal to the courts only in cases where the victim of the lynching was believed to have been guilty of no wanton crime.[30]

The various distinctions made between the white and colored races made necessary the definition of a person of color. George Johnstone argued for the definition of such a person as one who had any Negro blood. George Tillman, to the amazement of his hearers, asserted that "it is a scientific fact that there is no full-blooded Caucasian on the floor of this Convention."[31] His

[28] *Constitution,* Art. VI. Sec. 6.

[29] *News and Courier,* November 10, 1895.

[30] Congressman Fred H. Dominick said in 1922, "I think possibly three actions have been brought since that time (1895) under the law. . . . As far as lynching is concerned the provision of the Constitution had no more to do with it than if it were not there." *Congressional Record,* LXII. 1345.

[31] *News and Courier,* October 16, 1895.

words carried some weight, for when Johnstone's proposal was returned from the committee to which it was referred, it defined a person of color as "a person with one-eighth or more of negro blood." In this form it was adopted.[32]

In the consideration of questions which had no bearing on the race problem the convention acted in a spirit of wholesome progress. A new life was given to the educational provisions of the constitution of 1868. The property tax for schools was raised from two to three mills, to be distributed in proportion to the number of pupils enrolled. An annual poll tax on males and a portion of the Dispensary revenue were likewise assigned the schools. Tillman successfully advocated compact school districts of such size as to eliminate the necessity of the pupils' walking many miles to school. Although the effort to make it obligatory upon the legislature to support the state institutions of learning was defeated, Tillman was able to incorporate, over the opposition of the friends of denominational colleges, a provision prohibiting state subsidies to private institutions of learning.[33] Tillman, who was a champion of the small homestead, incorporated in the constitution a provision exempting homesteads to the value of

[32] *Convention Journal,* p. 342; *Constitution,* Art. III. Sec. 32.

[33] The debate on the educational provision is in the *News and Courier,* November 15, 16, 19, 1895; the votes, *Convention Journal,* pp. 561-2, 573; *Constitution,* Art. XI. Secs. 6, 9, 12.

$1500 each ($1000 in land and $500 in personal property) from the claims of the creditors of the owners, with the exception, of course, of debt incurred in purchase or through mortgage or taxation.[34] The fear that future legislatures might unduly extend the length of their sessions in order to increase their pay was satisfied by a provision that the *per diem* of the members should not run over forty days.[35] The proposal that South Carolina should abandon its unique position of not granting divorces and substitute a provision making adultery the one ground for divorce was defeated, due to the opposition of the religious sentiment of the state.[36] Even the influence of Tillman could not force the adoption of a provision recognizing the divorce decrees of other states.[37] The Dispensary was recognized by a provision giving the legislature power to grant a liquor monopoly to the state or to a designated private group. Yet Tillman deserves credit for not making impossible the abolition of that institution by simple legislative enactment, for the same provision gave the legislature power to enact Prohibition as the alternative of the Dis-

[34] *Constitution,* Art. III. Sec. 28.

[35] *Ibid.,* Art. XVIII. Sec. 3.

[36] As expressed in the *Southern Christian Advocate,* September 20, 1895, and *Baptist Courier,* September 23, 1895.

[37] *News and Courier,* September 27, 1895; *Convention Journal,* p. 258. Nevertheless the state Supreme Court has since recognized the legality of the divorce decrees granted in other states.

pensary system and only prohibited privately owned saloons.[38]

The convention gave much of its time to the consideration of means whereby new counties might be created. George Tillman, who from early youth had been an advocate of small units of local government, because they would serve to give the up-country a representation more in proportion to its population, and who had even advocated the introduction of the New England township scheme, came forward with a plan for the creation of as many counties as the individual communities of the state might elect, without limitation as to the minimum wealth, size, and population of the new units. However, he was brought to reason by a compromise offered by his brother, whereby counties could be readily created with a reasonable limit to their minimum size and taxable wealth.[39] In keeping with the increasing importance of the up-country, Charleston was deprived of one of its two senators.[40]

In deference to the desires of the two Tillmans, the convention, contrary to the usual practice of such assemblies, passed one act of specific legislation: a new county was created out of the Saluda

[38] *Convention Journal,* pp. 258, 299-330; *Constitution,* Art. XIII. Sec. 10. "We may have dispensaries; we may have Prohibition," said Tillman, "but there will never be another barroom in the state." *New York World,* October 2, 1895.

[39] *Constitution,* Art. VII. Secs. 7-10.

[40] *Ibid.,* Art. III. Sec. 8.

River section of Edgefield. The inhabitants of other areas who desired new counties were forced to await the action of the general constitutional process.[41]

The most tense moments of the convention grew out of the debates over the name of the new county. While Ben was absent to attend a sick daughter, George Tillman induced the assembly to adopt, by vote of seventy-six to sixty-four, the name of Butler in honor of the Edgefield family of that name. In the debate he paid high tribute to General M. C. Butler, expressed the fear that "it will be a long time before the equal of Butler will sit in the Senate from South Carolina," and asserted that Martin Gary had failed to have a monument erected to his memory in Edgefield because of "the suspicion of independentism in 1880."[42] When Ben Tillman read in the newspapers what had been done and said, he was very angry, because, in deference to the wishes of its inhabitants, he wished to call the new county Saluda and because his brother had cast aspersions upon him and Gary in the interest of Butler, whom he despised because of their quarrels in 1894. In such a spirit he arose in the convention on the following morning to ask that the name "Saluda" be inserted in the place of "Butler."

[41] *Ibid.*, Art. VII.

[42] This debate is in the *News and Courier*, September 15, 1895; the vote is in *Convention Journal*, p. 95.

While no one dared to interrupt him, he pronounced a fierce denunciation of Butler. "I am fighting," he said,

> to prevent the Convention from sending the news abroad that the reform Convention has rebuked the Legislature which has retired Butler. . . . I here say, and measure my words, that this last Butler has disgraced the name of Butler and made it a stench in the nostrils of every white man of South Carolina.

He next launched into an odious comparison between Gary and Butler. He told the story "of an eagle too noble to win success by picking at flies," of a hero who had faced black mobs and had been frustrated in his ambitions by Butler. "It was the sentiment of righteous indignation and wounded sentiment," he said, "which called down the wrath of the people on Butler for this." He then reproached his brother for his disparaging comparison and censured Irby, who had voted for Butler County, for accepting the inference that he as senator was likewise inferior to Butler. Finally, he scolded the conservative delegates. "Those of you," he said, "who have blundered into this movement, take warning that if you give us the point of the sword you will receive it back."

The reaction of the convention to this speech illustrates the remarkable influence of Tillman's personality. The conservative delegates, with the exception of his brother, could not muster sufficient courage to reply, in spite of the fact that Butler, a most eminent member of their faction, had been subjected to a dreadful denunciation in his absence.[43] George Tillman, however, reproached his brother for his words and begged the assembly not "to act like jumping jacks when the master pulls the cord in a Punch and Judy Show." Irby, shaking his fist at Ben, said what he pleased. "I throw it back in your teeth," he said, "that nothing M. C. Butler has ever done will disgrace the name of Butler. It will live when yours is dead and forgotten." But the convention, acting "like jumping jacks," by vote of eighty to fifty-four reversed its previous action.[44] Thus the new county was called Saluda.

The convention, after a session of twelve weeks, adjourned December 2. With the exception of the controversies over the naming of Saluda County and over a few minor points, it had been characterized by harmonious sessions. The delegates, pro-Tillman and anti-Tillman, had been united by the serious purposes of restricting the suffrage and bringing the constitutional law of the state in line with the progress of the times. When the convention adjourned, provision had

[43] In fact Tillman induced many of the conservatives to join him when three days later the convention by vote of 123 to 23 censured N. G. Gonzales for reflections on President Evans. *News and Courier,* September 20, 1895; *Convention Journal,* p. 158.

[44] This debate is in the *News and Courier* and Columbia *Daily Register,* September 17, 1895; the vote is in the *Convention Journal,* p. 114.

been made, over the opposition of the Negro delegates, for putting the document into effect January 1, 1896, without a popular referendum. That it registered very accurately the wants and the desires of the dominant element of South Carolina is proven by the fact that thirty years after its promulgation it still remains as the fundamental law of the state, although other monuments of Tillmanism have been destroyed in the changes of time.[45]

[45] For commentaries on the work of this convention see: D. D. Wallace, *Sewanee Review,* IV. 348 ff. (May, 1896); Amora N. Eaton, *American Law Review,* XXVI. 198 ff. (March, 1897); Frank Spigener, "The South Carolina Constitution of 1895," Columbia University, M. A. Essay, 1920.

CHAPTER X

THE AFTER EFFECTS OF TILLMANISM

It is the purpose of this concluding chapter to review the effects of Tillmanism upon the life of the state after Tillman, the work of the constitutional convention being completed, subordinated his interest in South Carolina to the larger issues which devolved upon him as United States senator and as one of the leaders of the national Democratic party. We shall indicate, first, the extent of his personal influence upon the politics of his state; second, the decline of this influence; third, the permanent effects of Tillmanism upon the political life of South Carolina; and fourth, his permanent contributions to the movement for education.

The first interference of Tillman in the politics of South Carolina after he became senator was not altogether successful. In 1896, he desired the election of Evans as his colleague in the Senate and the election of William H. Ellerbe as governor.[1] Although the people were thoroughly satisfied with the manner in which Tillman had

[1] Irby did not offer himself for reëlection, since he and Tillman had quarrelled because of his failure to achieve note in Washington and for personal reasons.

conducted himself in Washington and followed his desire concerning Ellerbe, they were unwilling to honor Evans further, in spite of Tillman's earnest pleas in his behalf. Evans failed by a narrow margin to receive the majority necessary for nomination in the first primary (first state-wide primary) and was defeated in the second primary by Earle, Tillman's old opponent.[2] This defeat did not indicate a lasting break in Tillman's grip upon the state, for he was to win many subsequent victories. It did indicate that there were limits to his influence, that the people were unwilling to gratify his will to the extent of nominating one whom they felt had two years before been put through the convention in a high-handed manner and whose election would really mean the violation of a cardinal principle of Tillmanism; viz., that the public offices should not be given to lawyers and to members of office-holding families.

The death of Senator Earle in 1897 gave Tillman an opportunity to retrieve his ill fortune of the previous year. Again Irby, who now had the temerity to oppose his former friend, were Evans and John L. McLaurin. Tillman took an active part in the canvass, opposing Irby but remaining neutral as regards the other two candidates. The

[2] Even Edgefield gave Earle a large majority. The story of the canvass of 1896 is told in the *News and Couirer* and Augusta *Chronicle,* May 10 to September 15, 1896.

primary resulted in the nomination of McLaurin by a vote thrice that of Evans and six times that of Irby.[3] However, the elevation of McLaurin was not as complete a victory for Tillman as perhaps the selection of Evans would have been, for McLaurin clearly was never so close to Tillman as Evans and was of a more independent disposition.

The campaign of 1900, in its several aspects, was a personal triumph for Tillman. He desired reëlection to the Senate, the endorsement of the Dispensary, and the election of his candidates for governor and lieutenant governor. The first of these ambitions was accomplished in a thorough fashion. The May convention of the Democratic party endorsed his policies in the Senate, with only one delegate in opposition, and elected him as the head of the state's contingent to the national Democratic convention with power to vote for whomever he saw fit among the presidential aspirants.[4] The second and third ambitions were accomplished by the election of Miles McSweeney, a champion of the Dispensary, as governor over James A. Hoyt, a Prohibitionist, who had the support of strong elements among the Baptists and Methodists, and of James H. Tillman, a son of George Tillman, as lieutenant governor over

[3] The vote is in the *News and Courier,* August 25, 1897.

[4] The proceedings of the convention are in the *News and Courier* and Columbia *State,* May 21-23, 1900.

Cole L. Blease, who had vied with Tillman's nephew for the support of the Tillmanites. Tillman himself, uneasy over the Dispensary, had taken an active part in the canvass.[5]

Meanwhile, the conduct of Senator McLaurin was not such as to please his colleague. Tillman demanded an exacting obedience from those whom he advanced politically, and McLaurin showed tendencies towards independent action. Tillman had, during his career as senator, demonstrated a fierce opposition to the policies of the Republicans; whereas McLaurin, cherishing a vision of industrial progress for the South like that of New England through the adoption of Republican measures, voted for the Hanna ship subsidy bill and for the treaty for the annexation of the Phillippines. In addition, Tillman, who had exalted notions of his own personal worth and who by this time had gained national fame as an exposer of corruption, believed that McLaurin had been corrupted.[6] The result was that Till-

[5] Characteristic of the manner in which he conducted the fight for the Dispensary were his remarks to a delighted audience at Barnwell. "You love your liquor and you are going to have it. You love it just as you do your girls." *News and Courier,* September 4, 1900.

[6] The suspicion of corruption was based on the fact that shortly after an eloquent speech against the Philippine treaty he voted for that measure (*Congressional Record,* XXXII. 638), and that he wrote a letter to a prominent official of the Standard Oil Company asking to be "generously supported" in his opposition to Tillman. McLaurin to John D. Archbold, May 29, 1902, Tillman Scrapbook, No. 8.

man, in characteristic style, accused McLaurin of being a "betrayer of the people who should join the Republican party" and who "had no principles."[7] This was followed by the aceptance by Tillman of a challenge from McLaurin that both resign in order that they might test their strength before the people by standing for the same seat. But Governor McSweeney, on account of the ill health of McLaurin and disdainful of the wrath of Tillman, refused to accept the resignations, thereby depriving Tillman of the opportunity of burying the political future of his antagonist in an avalanche of votes.[8] McLaurin's political future, nevertheless, was ruined, for in 1902, after being barred from the primary by vote of the Democratic executive committee, he admitted the futility of a canvass against the "acknowledged dictator of South Carolina."[9]

The campaign of 1902 was another victory for Tillman. It was opened by one of his characteristic acts of decision. When State Senator Louis Appelt accused him of corruption, he rushed to Appelt's home in order to face his accuser in joint

[7] Tillman in the *News and Courier,* April 20, 1901.

[8] For the South Carolina phase of this controversy see the *News and Courier* and Columbia *State,* May 25, 27; June 1, 1902. The national phase of this controversy took the form of a fist fight between the two on the floor of the Senate on Washington's Birthday, 1902, growing out of Tillman's charge that "improper influences" had brought about McLaurin's change of front on the Philippine Treaty. *Congressional Record,* XXXV. 2081, 2087-89; Augusta *Chronicle,* February 23, 1902.

[9] *News and Courier,* May 5, 1902.

debate. The result was that he not only got a unanimous show of hands from the crowd to indicate its belief that he was innocent but also obtained from the discomfited Senator a retraction of his charges.[10] Tillman was able to effect the election of Asbury C. Latimer, described as an "inoffensive member of the Tillman movement," as McLaurin's successor in the Senate over the opposition of Evans and three prominent anti-Tillmanites.[11] Although he publicly made no choice among the candidates for governor, the election of Duncan C. Heyward, an aristocratic rice planter of the lowlands, over James H. Tillman, Jasper Talbert, and Martin F. Ansel, a Prohibitionist, was satisfactory to Tillman,[12] because Heyward favored the Dispensary.

[10] *News and Courier,* April 25, 1902.

[11] J. J. Hemphill, William Elliott, and D. S. Henderson.

[12] In reply to importunities that he endorse a candidate for governor, Tillman said that the "old lines had been obliterated" and that he did "not intend to turn a finger in behalf of any candidate." *News and Courier,* June 10, 1902.

The defeat of Lieutenant Governor James H. Tillman was due to the failure of his uncle to interest himself in his candidacy and to the charges which Gonzales brought against him. He was accused of being "a gambler, a liar and a drunkard," of "committing a fraud upon the Senate of the State by falsifying its records," and of stealing some of the funds of the Edgefield Monument Association. (Columbia *State,* July 28; August 8, 1902). Cherishing the belief that he would have been elected but for the opposition of Gonzales (Circular Letter of James H. Tillman, August 29, 1902), on January 15, 1903, four and one half months after the election, he shot the editor on the streets of Columbia in open daylight. He was later acquitted by a Lexington county jury on a plea of self-defense. A report of the trial is in the Columbia *State,* September 10 to October 15, 1903.

But this was the last time in which Tillman may be said to have exercised dictatorial control of the politics of the state. Although he was able to retain his own seat in the Senate in the decisive elections of 1906 and 1912, in both these years men whom he opposed were elected to the office of governor. The question which arises at this point is, why was Tillman's influence in state politics weakening?

In the first place, there was a vast difference between the Tillman before 1900 and the Tillman of later years. The former was an individual in the full vigor of manhood, ready to make his influence felt by a direct appeal to the voters; the latter an old man prevented by infirmity[13] from again making organized campaign speeches. The former was the agrarian agitator, the rebel against aristocracy and a conservative Democratic party; the latter was a defender of the Democratic administration at Washington and of the traditions of the United States Senate, and one anxious for the support of many conservative South Carolinians who had once been his enemies. It is not far from the truth to say that Tillman had outlived the Tillmanism of the nineties. Many of the "wool-hat boys," the men of little property and education, with strong notions of their indi-

[13] His first illness was in 1904, when he underwent an operation on the throat. In 1908 he suffered a stroke of paralysis, caused by the leakage of a blood vessel on the brain. He never again was able to exert himself strenuously in public speech.

vidual rights, had been supplanted by prosperous farmers and small business men of some education and with much stricter ideas of social discipline. What remained of the "wool-hat boys" were now cotton mill workers, with other than agricultural interests, who were following a different leader. The legislature was as much under the control of lawyers as it had been before the rise of Tillman.[14] The old program of agrarian reform was as dead as the Farmers' Alliance. Tillmanism was not likely to inspire those sentimental recollections usually associated even with movements of only historic significance. The memories of Tillmanism were unpleasant to most South Carolinians, for they recalled the quarrels of brothers, violent denunciations of many things that were held sacred; they evoked no reminiscences of battles lost or won, or of the gentlemen of the old school of the type which southerners revere. With Tillman's personality had been associated no warm sentiments; along with the respect for his sterling personal qualities, went the memory of the fact that he had been dictatorial and selfish, that he had quarrelled with his friends,[15] and, in

[14] In 1925 the lawyers greatly outnumbered the farmers in both house (47 members gave law as their only occupation and 38 gave farming as their only occupation); in 1885, as evidenced in chapter iii, note 16, the farmers greatly outnumbered the lawyers. See *House* and *Senate Journals,* 1925.

[15] *E.g.,* Talbert, Sampson Pope, George Tillman, McLaurin, Irby, and Blease.

B. R. Tillman
June 1910

the opinion of some,[16] had betrayed his old friends in order to receive the support of his former enemies. Little wonder the state has turned to Hampton instead of Tillman as the person to hold in esteem second to Calhoun.

Tillman, as we have already indicated,[17] lost the campaign of 1906, which was fought over the Dispensary, due to the fact that the independent and drink loving constituency of 1890 had largely been supplanted by a constituency more sober and better disciplined. He lost the campaign of 1912 because of the emergence of Cole L. Blease, an old Tillmanite, who now threatened Tillman's leadership of the politics of the state. Blease, after 1890, was an active Tillman partisan; in 1900 he became known throughout the state as the champion of such darker phases of Tillmanism as opposition to the Negro and compulsory education. Like Tillman, his political strength came from his direct appeals to the people, and he was a very clever imitator of Tillman's campaign methods. Tillman viewed with satisfaction his elevation to the governorship in 1910.[18] But Blease was no Ellerbe or McSweeney; he was a positive personality bent upon the gratification of his personal ambitions and representative of forces not taken

[16] *E.g.*, Blease, McLaurin, and Talbert at the time of the election of 1912.

[17] See above, chapter viii.

[18] Tillman in that year spoke from the same platform as Blease.

into account by Tillmanism. He was a townsman and a lawyer whose early popularity came from his associations in his father's hotel and livery stable. He was strongest, not among the farmers, but among the cotton mill workers, a class which had increased in strength with the industrialization of the state. His conduct as governor was more like that of a sensational demagogue than that of the agrarian politician of an earlier day responsible to conservative taxpaying farmers. In the face of criticisms and social snubs like those visited upon Tillman, he threw discretion to the winds; he pardoned great batches of convicts; he hurled imprudent words at the men and institutions he did not like and warned his opponents that, if defeated, he would, during his remaining months as governor, make them "sweat blood."[19] This conduct provoked Tillman to denounce Blease. "The State's good name," Tillman said, "has been made a byword and a hissing by the representations of its Governor."[20] Nevertheless, Blease was elected by a small majority.[21] This was possible because he had developed extraordinary power as a stump speaker,

[19] Blease tells the story of his life in his "Final Message to the General Assembly," *House Journal,* 1914, pp. 8-20. It must be said to his credit that his administrations were characterized by no financial abuses and that there is no evidence on which to base charges that he accepted money for any of the many pardons he granted.

[20] "The Ferguson Letter," Columbia *State,* August 24, 1912.

[21] Columbia *State,* August 28, 1912.

imitating Tillman in manners, because of his appeals to the white masses against corporations and the Negro, and because his audacious manners and acts made him the idol of a considerable element of the population which still liked such behavior. Although he has been defeated for public office no less than four times since 1912, he has been able to retain an iron hold upon more than forty per cent. of the Democratic voters of the state and was able in 1924 to win the seat in the United States Senate which Tillman held until his death in 1918.

Nevertheless, the Tillman movement made lasting contributions to the political life of South Carolina. Tillman taught the white democracy how to exercise a greater degree of control over the political affairs of the state than it had previously done, and he gave it a more direct method of exercising this control. Without these reforms the achievement of Prohibition would have been difficult, and Blease's victories most likely would never have taken place.

The means through which this control could be better exercised was the direct primary for the nomination of public officials. The adoption of the direct primary has meant the measurement of the political strength of the various counties of the state in direct proportion to the number of white voters in the counties instead of in proportion to the population, as had been the case under the convention system of nominations—a change which has made the will of the average white voter of the white counties of the up-country equal to that of the average white voter of the black counties of the low-country. The direct primary, as its name indicates, is a means through which the average voter can directly and secretly express his choice without the necessity of attending open club meetings, and perhaps of having his expression of will nullified by the machinations of politicians in the process of county and state conventions. In addition, the direct primary, as the most unhampered means through which the white masses could express their will, offered the minimum opportunity for discontent with the decisions of the Democratic party, which might lead to bolts of such a nature as to endanger white supremacy. Thus it is seen that there were sectional, class, and racial reasons for the adoption of the primary: the up-country desired to increase its strength; the white democracy wanted more direct control; and all classes of the whites desired to prevent a return of the Negro in politics.

The claim of Tillman that he was the one person most responsible for the primary in South Carolina has been challenged because of the fact that he was not a consistent advocate of that reform.[22] It cannot be denied that Tillman was no more the originator of the sectional motive for the primary than was he the originator of sectionalism itself. As a revival of the ante-bellum battle for increased representation for the back country, Pickens County had as early as 1876 adopted the primary for the nomination of its local officials, as had eight additional counties by 1878, and wellnigh all the counties by 1886—the time when Tillman first made his influence felt in state politics. As early as 1878 the newspapers of Anderson and Edgefield carried on a campaign against the alleged over-representation of Charleston in the Democratic convention. In 1886 it was not Tillman, but James L. Orr who fought for a state primary.[23] In addition, it should be remembered that Tillman did not advocate the primary as an abstract principle of justice or democracy. He was in favor of it when it served his immediate purposes and in opposition when it did not. As we have had occasion to indicate, he refused to institute the primary in 1890, 1892, and 1894, after he had gained control of the Democratic party, because as a political realist he knew that his faction possessed a political machine even more capable of manipulating the convention process than did the conservatives. In fact, the primary was not adopted until 1896,

[22] W. W. Ball in Snowden, *History of South Carolina,* II. 1027.
[23] *News and Courier,* August 11, 1886.

two years after Tillman was securely seated in the United States Senate.

Nevertheless, the fact remains that the achievement of the concrete aims of Tillmanism meant the advancement of the primary system, for the same sectional, class, and racial interests which were responsible for Tillmanism were likewise responsible for this system. Hence, in both Democratic conventions of 1888, as we have noted, Tillman was the vehement and unsuccessful advocate of this manner of nomination, against the opposition of the same conservatives who two years later were to exchange positions with him. He favored the primary at this time because he knew that it would increase the strength of the white masses and the up-country, where his greatest power lay. Although he had won the victories of 1890, 1892, and 1894 by the convention methods, practical considerations led to the adoption of the primary in 1896. A promise was thereby kept; even greater strength was given to the white masses among whom he was still strongest; and there was fear that a continuation of the convention system, which had fallen in disrepute through his agitations, would give pretext for insurgent movements, like those of 1890 and 1894, of such a nature as to endanger the supremacy of the white race. Likewise, it should be remembered that the state primary was never advocated by the anti-Tillman elements before it was adopted except in 1890, 1892, and 1894, when it was the only alternative to certain defeat, and that the convention system, because it gave the best opportunity to political experience and to the low-country, had been responsible for the defeat of Tillmanism in 1886 and 1888.

But perhaps of greater significance in the history of the progress of democracy in South Carolina than a mere provision of a means for a more adequate expression of public sentiment, was the fact that Tillman taught the people how to exercise the political power they already had. He won a greater victory for democracy in the Democratic conventions of 1888, when he forced the adoption of the principle of joint debates between candidates, than he would have won had he been able to force the adoption of the state primary. Making the most of this opportunity, he aroused the people to such a degree through his peculiar genius as a public speaker that they have ever since taken an active and decisive part in political affairs.[24] There can be little doubt that today, some thirty years after Tillman's agitations, the white majority still practice the habit of deter-

[24] For example, in South Carolina in 1912, 140,376 males out of a total white population of 679,161 voted in the primary, or 20 per cent.; in the same year only 15,010,257 persons in the United States out of a total population of 91,972,266 voted in the presidential election, or 16 per cent.

mining the policies of the state government which he taught them.

In addition to his permanent influence upon the political life of his state, Tillman has left Clemson and Winthrop Colleges as monuments to his career. "We do not propose," said Governor Tillman to the 424 students assembled at the opening of Clemson College, July 11, 1893, "to make one-sided, one-horse men of you, but you must work."[25] The dairy, shops, farms, and laboratory which he inspected that day gave certain evidence that the young men were to be taught to work intelligently at a minimum cost to their parents and to the state. With the expansion of housing capacity and the addition of other lines of study and research, the enrollment of students today is thrice that of 1893; and the institution, through its extension department, has given the farmers of the state the very information of which Tillman so keenly felt the need of in 1884.[26]

Of equal importance in promoting the progress of South Carolina has been the service of Win-

[25] *News and Courier,* July 12, 1893.

[26] Nevertheless, in view of the fact that the institution was founded for the purpose of educating farmers, it is to be regretted that so few of its students, although sons of farmers, return to the soil. For example, a study of the occupations of the 382 who had graduated in the ten-year period preceding 1906 (occupations given in *The Catalogue of Clemson College, 1906-1907,* pp. 161-184) reveals the fact that only 37 were in 1906 engaged in agriculture. However, these figures should not be interpreted as evidence of the college's inefficiency, but as evidence that the graduates have found non-agricultural callings more remunerative.

throp College. During the thirty years of its operation its enrollment has increased from 304 to 1580 students. At a minimum cost—$126.50 per year for each student in 1896—it has afforded an education to several thousand daughters of farmers and townsmen who but for its existence would have been unable to bear the expenses of a college education, and it has furnished the homes and schools of the state with women competently trained in domestic economy and pedagogy.[27]

From what has been said in the foregoing pages, it may be truly said that when Tillman died at Washington, July 3, 1918, he left a memory which will not soon be effaced from South Carolina history. His outstanding quality was his ability to foresee the inevitability of a revolution in the political control of the state and his ability to give direction to this change—this, although he was handicapped by a disagreeable personality, which led him to victory by the most difficult road and with the greatest amount of irritation to his opponents. Nevertheless, he possessed wisdom, honesty, restraint, and capacity sufficient to overcome personal handicaps. The result is that Tillmanism is still a reality in South Carolina. Through it the white democracy knows how to exercise control of the

[27] In 1925, 31 per cent. of its students were daughters of farmers, and there were 1739 former students teaching in the schools of the state. Winthrop dispatch to press of the state, April 6, 1925.

state's politics and has been given means through which the possibility of a return of the black democracy to power has been made very remote. Two industrial colleges for the education of the white youth of the state have been established. For twenty or more years the state had a forceful leader, and now it can cherish the memory of a rugged and picturesque personality, the like of whom South Carolina, which is losing is distinctive characteristics, is not likely to produce again. The state has learned to forget many of the actualities of Tillman's day; it is better educated and has a better sense of social discipline; but it may live to regret the passing of that uniqueness which made Tillman a success; it may never again produce so distinctive an individual.

BIBLIOGRAPHY

I—Manuscript

Order Books, Deed Books and Will Books found in the offices of the Clerk of Court and Probate Judge of Edgefield County.
They throw light upon the genealogy and business transactions of the Tillman family.

Records of Land Grants in the office of the Secretary of State of South Carolina and the Records of Militia Service in the office of the Secretary of the Historical Commission of South Carolina.
They throw light upon the Tillman ancestry.

Tillman, Benjamin R., Letters. Tillman Library, Trenton, and State Capitol, Columbia.
There is no collection of Tillman letters. Tillman seldom kept copies. Use has been made of the few found among the Tillman papers and those gathered from his correspondents. The correspondence of the governors of South Carolina was, by order of Governor Blease, thrown in a huge pile in the basement of the State Capitol, from which position no one has seen fit to recover it. Such letters of Governor Tillman as could be gleaned from this confusion have been utilized.

Tillman, Benjamin R., Manuscripts. Tillman Library, Trenton.
This material is characterized by frank confessions. While it contains inaccuracies, the papers are sprightly and full of keys to motives. They are:
(a) "My Childhood Days," the first and only chapter of a proposed autobiography.

(b) "The Story of Clemson," a narration of the conferences connected with the origin of the agricultural college.

(c) "The Darlington Riot," an account of Tillman's motives during the "Dispensary War."

(d) Numerous statements of personal philosophy pasted in the Tillman Scrapbooks.

Tillman, Benjamin Ryan, Sr., The Diary of.
A record of family affairs and personal accounts kept by Tillman's father.

Walmsley, J. E., Causes and Early History of Tillmanism.
A paper in the possession of the present writer by a close student of South Carolina history chiefly concerned with the economic background of Tillmanism.

Youmans, Laurence, Note Book, Tillman Library, Trenton.
The story of the campaign of 1892 by one of Tillman's opponents.

II—Documents

Acts and Joint Resolutions of the General Assembly of the State of South Carolina. Columbia, 1873——.

Butler, A. P., *South Carolina. Resources and Population, Institutions and Industries.* Columbia, 1883.
A compilation by the commissioner of agriculture.

Census of the United States, *Reports.* Washington, 1790——.
Serviceable for facts on the distribution of wealth and for an understanding of inter-racial problems.

Clemson College Bulletin. A Quarterly. Clemson College, 1894——.
Reports of the researches of the agricultural and mechanical college.

Congressional Record. Washington, 1873——.
Contains the record of Tillman while in the United States Senate.

Constitution of the State of South Carolina . . . Adopted by the Constitutional Convention which was held at Charleston, and adjourned on the 17th March, 1868. Charleston, 1868.

Constitution of the State of South Carolina, 1895, ratified in Convention December 4 in *Code of Laws of South Carolina, 1912,* II. 595-656. Charlottesville, Virginia, 1912 (Cited as *Constitution*).

Cooper, Thomas and McCord, Davis, J., *The Statutes at Large of South Carolina.* Columbia, 1836-41.

Davis, J. C. Bancroft, *Cases Argued and Adjudged in the Supreme Court* (U. S. Supreme Court Reports), 79 Vols. etc., Boston, 1876-1902.

Useful for decisions concerning the litigation over the Dispensary.

Federal Reporter. St. Paul, 1880——.

House Executive Documents. Washington, 1847——; *House Miscellaneous Documents,* Washington, 1847——; *House Reports of Committees,* Washington, 1819——.

The publications of Congress throw intimate light upon the numerous contested elections of South Carolina and upon the activities of Tillman as manager of elections and participiant in riots.

Journal of the Convention of the people of South Carolina, held in Columbia, S. C., September, 1865. Columbia, 1865.

A mere record of procedure.

Journal of the Constitutional Convention of the People of South Carolina held at Columbia, S. C., beginning September 10th and ending December 4th, 1895. Columbia, 1895. (Cited as *Convention Journal*).

A mere record of events, except for Tillman's most important speech and the reply of the Negro delegates to it. It is understandable only in connection with the debates as published in the *News and Courier.*

Journal of the House of Representatives of the State of South Carolina. Columbia, 1873——. (Cited as *House Journal*).

Journal of the Senate of the State of South Carolina. Columbia, 1873——. (Cited as *Senate Journal*).

Annual publications best understood in connection with the legislative debates published in the *News and Courier.*

Proceedings of the Constitutional Convention of South Carolina, held at Charleston, S. C., beginning January 14th and ending March 17th, 1868. Charleston, 1868.

A full record of the debates and procedure of this most interesting assemblage.

Report of the Joint Legislative Committee on Frauds (The). Columbia, 1877.

The testimony and report of a Democratic legislative committee presenting the evidence of Republican fraud during Reconstruction.

Reports and Resolutions of the General Assembly of the State of South Carolina. Columbia, 1873——.

This official publication of the state contains the annual reports of the heads of departments of the state government, together with the testimony of the legislative committees that investigated the Dispensary, 1905-1909.

Reports of Cases heard and determined by the Supreme Court of South Carolina. Columbia, 1868——.

This publication is especially useful for the decisions of the Supreme Court concerning the litigation over the Dispensary.

South Carolina Legislative Times (The), 33rd Leg., 2nd Session. Columbia, 1856.

The only stenographic report of a South Carolina legislative session known to the author. Used for a speech of George Tillman.

III. Periodicals (Newspapers, Magazines, and Annual Publications)

Tillman was a subject of so much discussion in South Carolina periodicals and was so frequently in newspaper controversies that it has been necessary to examine the leading South Carolina journals page by page for the period of his activity.

Advertiser (The). Edgefield, 1836——.

Valuable for the local history of the county of the Tillman family. Strongly anti-Republican and pro-Tillman.

American Annual Cyclopedia. N. Y., 1861-1902.

The articles on South Carolina are used for history of the state between 1876 and 1885.

American (The). Charleston, 1917-23.

This newspaper was the pro-Blease daily.

Agricultural and Mechanical Society of South Carolina, *Proceedings.* Columbia, 1869——.

A record of the work of the most conservative of the post-bellum agricultural societies.

Daily Register (The). Columbia, 1884-1897.

After February, 1892, this newspaper was the unofficial mouthpiece of the Tillman administration and the only daily not hostile. Its subsidy was the public printing. Notable for the sprightly editorials of T. Larry Gantt.

Baptist Courier (The). Greenville, 1869——.

The unofficial publication of the most powerful and most numerous religious group in the state. It was hostile to Tillman and the Dispensary.

Brandenburg, Broughton, "Tillman at Home," *The Delineator,* February, 1908. N. Y., 1868——.

An intimate picture of Senator Tillman at home, by an experienced reporter of a New York fashion magazine.

Chronicle (The). Augusta, Ga., 1785——.

Interested in South Carolina affairs, this border daily has a balanced view.

Chronicle (The). Edgefield, 1881-1925.
Valuable for the opinions of its talented anti-Tillman editor, James T. Bacon. It contains records of Tillman's earliest efforts on behalf of agricultural education.

Dargan, W. F., *see* Tillman.

Eaton, Amora N., "The New Constitution of South Carolina," *American Law Review,* XXVI (Feb., 1896). St. Louis, 1866——.
A criticism of the work of the convention from a purely legal viewpoint.

Flisch, Julia A., "Discontent in the Old South," American Historical Association, *Annual Report, 1908,* I, 133-142. Washington, 1890——.
An inadequate record of white discontent before 1861 in the South.

Gould, E. R. L., "The Gothenburg Plan," *Atlantic Monthly,* LXXII (Feb., 1894). Boston, 1857——.
A history of the institution on which the Dispensary was modeled.

Herald and News (The). Newberry, 1865——.
Anti-Tillman and pro-Blease bi-weekly.

Journal of Negro History (The). Washington, 1916——.
Contains useful documents on Reconstruction.

Keowee Courier. Walhalla, 1849——.
A country weekly of the mountains of South Carolina.

Koester, George R., See *Greenville Piedmont.*

McCrady, Edward, "Slavery in the Province of South Carolina, 1670-1770," American Historical Association, *Annual Report,* 1895, pp. 631-673. Washington, 1890——.
This publication describes the condition of the lower classes and the origin of the indentured servant.

Nation (The). New York, 1865——.
Vol. I is used for the report of J. R. Dennett concerning conditions in South Carolina during the summer and fall of 1865.

News and Courier (The). Charleston, 1803——.
This newspaper is the greatest single source of information used by the author. N. G. Gonzales in its columns covered the political and social life of the state during the period of Tillman's activity and was present at all the meetings of the canvasses of 1888 and 1890. It had as its editor the brilliant Englishman, Francis W. Dawson, who, though hostile to Tillman, was always fair. In its files are contained the series of letters which first gave Tillman notoriety. Under Dawson and his immediate successors it dominated the new service of the state—a privilege which it exercised with moderation.

News and Herald (The). Winnsboro, 1844——.
An alert country weekly, hostile to Tillman.

News (The). Greenville, 1874——.
This daily represented the industrial interests of the Piedmont and was hostile to Tillman. Its able editor was A. B. Williams.

New York Newspapers. *The American.* N. Y., 1882-——; *The Herald.* N. Y., 1835——; *The Times.* N. Y., 1851——; and *The World.* N. Y., 1860——.
Contain interesting articles on South Carolina affairs written by outsiders.

Piedmont (The). Greenville, 1824——.
Used for a series of editorial recollections appearing in 1916 by George R. Koester, who, in 1892, was a reporter of the *Register* and a confidant of Tillman. While he exaggerates his own importance, he is fair.

Record, (The). Columbia, 1897——.
Valuable for hostile comments on Blease.

Rural Carolinian (The). Charleston, 1885-1894.
The journal of the conservative agricultural interests.

Schaper, William, "Sectionalism and Representation in South Carolina," American Historical Association, *Annual Report, 1900,* I. 237-463. Washington, 1890 ——.

This is a most valuable discussion of the social and industrial bases of sectionalism in South Carolina, the understanding of which is necessary to explain the post-bellum sectionalism.

Simkins, Francis B., "The Election of 1876 in South Carolina," *South Atlantic Quarterly,* XXI-XXII (October 1922-January 1923). Durham, N. C., 1902——.

A narration of events crucial in the post-bellum history of the state.

Simkins, Francis B., "The Negro in South Carolina Law since 1865," *Ibid.,* XXI (March-July, 1922).

A study of the reflection of racial discriminations in the statutes of the state.

Southern Christian Advocate (The). Columbia, 1837——.

The official publication of the second strongest religious group in South Carolina, the Methodist Episcopal Church, South. Hostile to Tillman and the Dispensary.

State (The). Columbia, 1891——.

This newspaper was founded by N. G. Gonzales shortly after his resignation from the *News and Courier,* in order that he might be unhampered in his relentless battle against Tillman. Beginning with hardly more than a daily tirade against Tillman, it soon equalled the *News and Courier* as a reporter of the happenings of the state. After the death of Gonzales (1903), it became more moderate in its hostility to Tillman.

State Agricultural Society of South Carolina, *Proceedings.* Columbia, 1839-1845.

A record of the most notable ante-bellum organization of this nature.

Sun (The). Charleston, 1889-1894.

A daily somewhat opposed to Tillman. Its only available file, a volume of 1890, is in the library of the Charleston Library Association.

Tillman Scrapbooks. 12 Vols. Tillman Library, Trenton, 1885-1919.

This collection contains thousands of unclassified clippings from the press of the state and the nation.

Tillman, Benjamin R., "The South Carolina Law" and "Our Whisky Rebellion." *North American Review,* CLVIII (April, 1894 and June, 1894).

Tillman, Benjamin R., and Dargan, W. F., "A Last Word on the South Carolina Liquor Law," CLIX, *Ibid.* (July, 1894).

These articles contain a defence of Governor Tillman's action in the suppression of the "Whisky Rebellion," with a reply from a citizen of Darlington.

University Carolinian (The). Columbia, 1883——.

A publication of the students of the University of South Carolina. It is interesting for its comments on the reforms made by Tillman in the organization of the university.

Virginia Magazine of History and Biography (The). Richmond, 1893——.

Useful for the tracing of the Tillman genealogy.

Wallace, David Duncan, "The South Carolina Constitution of 1895," *Sewanee Review,* IV (Nov., 1896). Sewanee, Tenn., 1892——.

The comments of a scholarly South Carolinian on the convention.

Watchman and Southron (The). Sumter, 1850——.

A bi-weekly hostile to Tillman.

World Almanac and Book of Facts (The). N. Y., 1886——.

World (The). Charleston, 1889-91.

The first pro-Tillman daily. Its files contain full accounts of the political happenings of 1890.

Yorkville Enquirer (The). York, 1855——.

A pro-Tillman and pro-Blease bi-weekly.

IV.—Works On South Carolina History (Narratives and Biographies)

ALLEN, WALTER, *Governor Chamberlain's Administration in South Carolina.* N. Y., 1888.
The able and full apology of the last Republican governor of South Carolina.

CALHOUN, JOHN C., *Works,* (Edited by P. K. Crallé), 6 Vols. N. Y., 1853-55.

CHAPMAN, JOHN A., *History of Edgefield County.* Newberry, 1902.
This is the only history of the community from which the Tillmans came. It is composed of laudatory recollections of families admired by the author. No attempt is made to consult or organize facts. Its only hostile paragraphs are directed against the Tillmans.

COOK, OLIVER T., *Life and Legacy of David R. Williams.* N. Y., 1916.
A thorough but diffuse life of a notable ante-bellum industrialist and Baptist.

Descriptive Review of South Carolina. Columbia, 1893.
A compilation containing many valuable biographical facts.

GREEN, EDWIN L., *A History of the University of South Carolina.* Columbia, 1916.
A careful history based on the minutes of the board of trustees and the author's intimate association with the institution. It avoids unpleasant incidents in the post-bellum history of the university.

GUNTER, U. X., JR., *The Dispensary Law as Digested from the Code of 1902.* Columbia, 1903.
A work of the assistant attorney general of South Carolina.

JONES, IRA B., *Cornerstone Address.* Rock Hill, May 12, 1894.
The work of one closely identified with the early history of the South Carolina woman's college.

JOYNES, EDWARD S., *Origin and Early History of Winthrop.* Rock Hill, no date. Among *South Carolina Pamphlets,* Library of the University of South Carolina.
A pamphlet by one closely associated with the founding of the South Carolina woman's college.

LANDRUM, J. O. B., *A Colonial and Revolutionary History of Upper South Carolina.* Greenville, 1897.
Useful for the early history of the Piedmont.

LELAND, JOHN A., *A Voice from South Carolina.* Charleston, 1879.
An attack on the Reconstruction government.

MILLS, ROBERT, *Statistics of South Carolina.* Charleston, 1823.
A description of social and economic South Carolina around 1820. It is of special use for its description of Edgefield.

MCCRADY, EDWARD, JR., AND ASHE, SAMUEL A., *Cyclopedia of Eminent and Representative Men of the Carolinas of the Nineteenth Century.* 2 Vols. Madison, 1892.
Volume one is valuable for its biographies of notable South Carolinians.

MERIWETHER, COLYER, *The History of Higher Education in South Carolina.* Washington, 1889.

MILLER, MRS. THOMAS J., *Speeches of the Negro Delegates Before the Constitutional Convention of 1895.* No imprint or date.
By the wife of a Negro delegate.

O'NEALL, J. BELTON, *Biographical Sketches of the Bench and Bar of South Carolina.* Charleston, 1859.
The work of a most notable jurist of ante-bellum South Carolina, who compiled interesting facts concerning the state's most notable jurists and lawyers.

PIKE, JAMES SHEPPARD, *The Prostrate State: South Carolina under Negro Government.* N. Y., 1874.
A graphic description of the follies of Negro rule.

REYNOLDS, JOHN S., *Reconstruction in South Carolina.* Columbia, 1905.

The careful record of a southern partisan.

SEABROOK, W. P., *An Essay on the Agricultural Capabilities of South Carolina.* Columbia, 1839.

A critical analysis by a eminent citizen of the agricultural future of the state.

SNOWDEN, YATES (editor), *History of South Carolina.* 5 Vols. Chicago, 1920.

Volumes I and II constitute the only attempt, aside from school primers, which has been made to narrate the whole history of the state. The sections concerning more recent history are not appreciative of Tillman. Volumes III, IV, and V are composed of biographies of contemporary South Carolinians. Although extravagant, they contain many useful facts.

SPIGENER, FRANK, "The South Carolina Constitutional Convention of 1895," M. A. Essay in the Library of Columbia University.

An interpretation of material to which the author of the present work had access.

TILLMAN, B. R., *Address before the Democratic Convention of May 13, 1918.* Columbia, 1918.

TILLMAN, B. R., *The Struggle of 1876, Being the Story of the Red Shirt Movement.* Anderson, 1909.

Valuable for the story of Tillman's part in Reconstruction and for his exposure of the motives of his party.

TOWNE, LAURA M., *Letters and Diary.* Cambridge, 1912.

The record of a New England Abolitionist's venture as a mistress of a successful Negro school. Her associations with Negro politicians are recorded.

WALKER, C. IRVINE, *A History of the Agricultural Society of South Carolina.* Charleston, 1919.

A critical appreciation of the efforts of the planters of the Charleston district by the official historian of the society.

V—Works Not Specially Concerned With South Carolina

Andrews, Sidney, *The South Since the War.* N. Y., 1866.
Valuable for intimate pictures of Reconstruction leaders and for descriptions of social conditions in South Carolina.

Blakey, Leonard Scott, "The Sale of Liquor in the South," *Columbia University Studies in History, Economics, and Public Law,* LI (1912). N. Y., 1897——.
Valuable for its collection of facts on the state Dispensary.

Buck, Solon J., *The Granger Movement.* Cambridge, 1913.
A definitive history of the national organization, with ample facts on its South Carolina branches.

Buck, Solon J., *The Agrarian Crusade.* New Haven, 1921.
Used for its chapters on the Farmers' Alliance.

Chamberlain, H. R., *The Farmers' Alliance.* N. Y., 1891.
A contemporary history of this movement. Uncritical.

Fanshowe, E. L., *A History of Liquor Legislation in the United States.* London, 1894.
This English author visited South Carolina to investigate the enforcement of the Dispensary law.

Fleming, Walter L., *Documentary History of Reconstruction.* 2 Vols. Cleveland, 1906-07.

Helper, Hinton R., *The Impending Crisis of the South: How to Meet It.* N. Y., 1857.
An unfavorable criticism of the social conditions among the non-slave-holding classes of the South which throws light on conditions in South Carolina.

Herbert, H. A., *Why the Solid South? Or, Reconstruction and its Results.* Baltimore, 1890.

An apology for the South's reactionary policy toward the Negro, containing a chapter devoted to South Carolina by J. J. Hemphill, congressman from South Carolina. It is interesting for the views of conservative South Carolinians on the race problem.

MORGAN, W. SCOTT, *History of the Wheel and Alliance.* N. Y., 1891.

A contemporary history of the Alliance. Uncritical.

NATIONAL ASSOCIATION FOR THE ADVANCEMENT OF COLORED PEOPLE, THE. *Thirty Years of Lynching in the United States.* N. Y., 1920.

This publication contains an incomplete list of lynchings in South Carolina, 1889-1919.

National Cyclopedia of American Biography (The). N. Y., 1893——.

This work contains many facts conveniently arranged concerning notable South Carolinians.

Negro in the United States, 1790-1915 (The). Washington, 1918.

A convenient collection from the census concerning the Negro.

OLMSTEAD, FREDERICK LAW, *A Journey in the Seaboard Slave States in the Years 1853-1854.* New ed., N. Y., 1904.

This scientist made careful observations concerning the plantation system and condition of the poor whites in ante-bellum South Carolina.

OTKIN, CHARLES H., *The Ills of the South; Or, Relating Causes Hostile to the General Prosperity of the Southern People.* N. Y., 1894.

An explanation from the pen of an agrarian agitator of why the southern farmers were dissatisfied.

PECK, HARRY THURSTON, *Twenty Years of the Republic, 1885-1905.* N. Y., 1907.

A narrative of the history of the United States during the period of Tillman's greatest activity, which is notable for a graphic description of the man.

PHILLIPS, ULRICH B., *American Negro Slavery*. N. Y., 1918.

A thorough description of the slave plantation with ample reference to South Carolina.

RHODES, JAMES FORD, *A History of the United States since the Compromise of 1850*. 9 Vols. N. Y., 1893-1922.

South in the Building of the Nation (The). 13 Vols. Richmond, 1909-13.

This attempt to present the South's contributions to American history contains, in Vols. V and VI, many facts concerning the social and economic history of South Carolina.

THOMPSON, HOLLAND, *The New South*. New Haven, 1921.

A history of the social and political conditions of the South since Reconstruction, with sections on South Carolina.

INDEX